CURRIED AND SPICED

CHARMAINE SOLOMON

HAMLYN

Published 1993 by Hamlyn Australia,
a part of Reed Books Australia
22 Salmon Street, Port Melbourne, Victoria 3207
a division of Reed International Books Australia Pty Limited

Photographs by Rodney Weidland
Styling by Margaret Alcock
Food cooked by Jill Pavey, Romany de Silva, Deborah Solomon
China Queen's Plate by Wedgwood, Hand Crafted Ceramic Ware from
Studio Showcase, Rozelle, NSW
Typeset in 9½ on 12pt Berkeley Old Style Book by Midland Typesetters
Produced in Hong Kong by Mandarin Offset

National Library of Australia
    cataloguing-in-publication data:

Solomon, Charmaine.
    Curried and spiced.

    Includes index.
    ISBN 0 947334 58 0.

    1. Cookery (curry). 2. Spices. 3. Cookery, Oriental. I. Title. (Series: Asian
cookery library).

641.6384

Introduction

The various herbs, spices and sauces used in Asian cooking can turn seemingly everyday ingredients into exciting, tongue-tingling dishes.

Until comparatively recently, a Western 'curry' comprised leftover roast and bore little resemblance to the traditional dish. Travel, immigration and the proliferation of Asian restaurants, however, have brought with them the authentic dish.

Not every spiced dish is a curry and in *Curried and Spiced* you will find many kinds of soups, stews, stir-fries, roasts and braised dishes. Here is your guide to using spices cleverly.

Seafood

There is a good mixture of dishes from Asian countries in this section. The large number of Thai recipes, however, no doubt reflects my preference for the imaginative, spicy flavours of Thai seafood.

Serve either as a zingy, bite-size cocktail savoury, each prawn in its spicy coating perched on a freshly fried crouton, or as a sambal with rice and other curries.

DEVILLED PRAWNS
Serves 4 to 6

- *500 g (1 lb) small to medium sized raw prawns*
- *2 tablespoons peanut oil*
- *2 onions, finely chopped*
- *3 cloves garlic, crushed*
- *1–2 teaspoons chilli powder*
- *1 teaspoon salt or to taste*
- *½ cup hot and sweet chilli sauce*

Shell and devein prawns. If wet, dry on kitchen paper. Heat oil in a wok or frying pan and cook onions and garlic over gentle heat until soft and translucent. When starting to brown add chilli powder and fry for a few seconds, then stir in salt, chilli sauce and prawns. Toss until prawns are cooked and sauce almost dry.

If you are able to buy fresh curry leaves and pandan leaves the flavour of this curry will be much better. These are becoming increasingly common in Asian shops.

Sri Lankan Fish Curry with Tamarind
Serves 4

- 4 cutlets of jewfish, Spanish mackerel or cod
- turmeric, salt and freshly ground black pepper
- oil for frying
- 2 sprigs fresh curry leaves or 20 dried
- 2 large onions, finely chopped
- 1 teaspoon fenugreek seeds
- 2 teaspoons finely chopped garlic
- 2 teaspoons finely grated fresh ginger
- 1 small stick cinnamon
- strip of fresh, frozen or dried pandan leaf
- 2 tablespoons Ceylon Curry Powder (see p. 79)
- 1 tablespoon dried tamarind pulp
- 1 cup canned coconut milk

Rub cutlets with turmeric, salt and pepper. In a large pan heat 3 tablespoons oil and on low heat fry curry leaves, onions, fenugreek seeds, garlic, ginger, cinnamon and pandan leaf until onions are soft and golden. Add curry powder and fry for 2 minutes, stirring.

Soak tamarind pulp in ½ cup hot water and when cool squeeze to dissolve pulp. Strain, discarding seeds and fibres. Add to pan. Stir in coconut milk mixed with ½ cup water and simmer, uncovered, until sauce thickens.

Put in fish steaks and spoon sauce over. Simmer for about 10 minutes. Serve hot with rice and vegetables.

THAI RED CURRY OF FISH
Serves 4 to 5

- *750 g (1½ lb) steaks or fillets of firm white fish*
- *1 teaspoon turmeric*
- *salt*
- *4 tablespoons peanut oil*
- *3 tablespoons Thai Red Curry Paste (see p. 80)*
- *4 shallots, finely chopped*
- *finely grated rind of 1 lime*
- *1 cup canned coconut milk*
- *4 kaffir lime leaves*
- *8 small red or green chillies*
- *2 tablespoons fish sauce*
- *1 tablespoon palm sugar*
- *juice of 1 lime or half lemon*
- *20–30 fresh basil leaves*

Rub fish with turmeric and salt and fry lightly in hot oil. In oil remaining in wok fry Red Curry Paste and shallots, stirring constantly, until fragrant. Add grated lime rind, coconut milk, 1 cup water, lime leaves, whole chillies, fish sauce and sugar. Simmer uncovered for 10 minutes.

Add fish steaks and continue simmering for a further 10 minutes. Stir in lime juice and basil leaves and serve at once with steamed rice and a vegetable dish, such as White Vegetable Curry (see p. 58) or Bean Sayur (see p. 54).

Even people who are not great fish eaters go for this flavoursome dish in a big way. Serve cut into wedges as an appetiser. Or it makes a light main dish for 4 with a salad of sliced cucumber and tomatoes dressed with lime juice and a pinch each of sugar and salt.

THAI STEAMED FISH PUDDING
Serves 6

- 500 g (1 lb) bream, sea perch or other white fish fillets
- 2 tablespoons fish sauce
- 1 tablespoon Thai Red Curry Paste (see p. 80)
- finely grated rind of 1 lime
- 1 teaspoon finely chopped lesser galangal
- 1 egg, lightly beaten
- ½ cup canned coconut milk
- ½ cup finely chopped spring onions
- small basil leaves
- seeded and sliced red chillies
- 2 kaffir lime leaves, finely shredded

TOPPING
- ¾ cup canned coconut milk
- 1 tablespoon rice flour
- ¼ teaspoon salt

Remove all traces of skin and any stray bones from fillets and dice fish. Put fish into food processor fitted with steel blade. Add rest of ingredients except spring onions. Process until mixture forms a paste, remove to a bowl and stir in onions.

Spread mixture in a round heatproof dish or pie plate and pour Topping over, spreading it to edges. Cover and steam over boiling water for 18 to 20 minutes. Allow to cool for a few minutes, then remove from steamer and garnish with basil leaves, chilli and lime leaves. Serve warm or cold.

TOPPING Combine coconut milk, rice flour and salt in a small pan and stir over medium heat until it boils and thickens.

For a dish which is so simple to make, the results are outstandingly tasty. If you are not really into hot flavours, use a sweet chilli sauce and hold back on the fresh chillies.

CHILLI PRAWNS
Serves 4

- *500 g (1 lb) large, raw prawns*
- *¼ cup peanut oil*
- *½ cup chopped spring onions*
- *2 teaspoons finely grated fresh ginger*
- *2 teaspoons crushed garlic*
- *2 or 3 red chillies, finely chopped*
- *¼ cup chilli sauce*
- *¼ cup tomato ketchup*
- *1 tablespoon sugar*
- *1 tablespoon light soy sauce*
- *salt to taste*

Shell and devein prawns, leaving only the tail on.

In a wok, heat oil and fry spring onions, ginger, garlic and chillies, stirring, until fragrant. Add chilli sauce and tomato ketchup, sugar, soy sauce and salt, stirring to dissolve sugar. Add prawns and toss in mixture until well coated and cooked through. Serve with steamed white rice.

Perhaps the best known of all Thai dishes, this fiery soup is a wonderful start to a meal for jaded palates.

Hot-Sour Prawn Soup
Serves 6

- 500 g (1 lb) small to medium raw prawns
- 1 tablespoon oil
- 1 teaspoon salt
- 2 or 3 stems fresh lemon grass, thinly sliced or thinly peeled rind of 1 lemon
- 4 fresh or frozen kaffir lime leaves
- 4 slices greater galangal, fresh, brined or frozen
- 4 fresh red chillies
- 3 teaspoons chopped garlic
- 2 tablespoons fish sauce
- 1 tablespoon palm sugar
- ¼ cup lime juice or more to taste
- ¼ cup chopped fresh coriander leaves
- ¼ cup sliced spring onions

Shell and devein prawns, saving heads and shells for making stock. Heat oil in a saucepan and fry heads and shells until they turn red. Add 2 litres water, salt, lemon grass, lime leaves, galangal, 3 of the chillies and garlic. Cover and simmer for 20 minutes, then strain stock.

Rinse saucepan and return stock. Add prawns and simmer for a few minutes, just until they turn opaque and curl. Add palm sugar, fish sauce and lime juice to taste, remove from heat and serve sprinkled with remaining chilli finely sliced, coriander and spring onions.

Everybody's favourite prawn dish. Leaving shells on retains great flavour, but remove intestinal tract by snipping it just above tail segment and carefully drawing it out where head meets body. Very anatomical and fiddly, but getting rid of the gritty bit adds to the enjoyment.

THAI PRAWNS WITH BASIL
Serves 6

- 750 g (1½ lb) large, raw prawns, deveined
- 2 tablespoons oil
- 3 tablespoons Thai Red Curry Paste (see p. 80)
- 1½ cups canned coconut milk
- 5 fresh, frozen or dried kaffir lime leaves
- finely grated rind of 1 lime
- 2 tablespoons fish sauce
- 1 tablespoon palm sugar
- 20–30 basil leaves

Heat oil in a wok or saucepan and fry Red Curry Paste over low heat, stirring constantly, until fragrant. Add 1 cup coconut milk and 1½ cups water, lime leaves, rind and fish sauce. Simmer, uncovered, for 10 minutes. Add prawns and remaining ½ cup coconut milk and cook, stirring and turning, for a further 10 minutes or until prawns are cooked. Stir in palm sugar until dissolved, and throw in basil leaves just before serving. Serve with steamed rice.

From the inland Chinese province of Szechwan comes this robustly flavoured fish dish.

Fish in Chilli Bean Sauce
Serves 4

- 2 whole white fish, about 750 g (1½ lb) each
- 2 teaspoons finely grated ginger
- 1 teaspoon salt
- ½ cup peanut oil
- 1 tablespoon finely chopped garlic
- 1 tablespoon finely chopped ginger
- 2 teaspoons chilli bean sauce or to taste
- 2 tablespoons dark soy sauce
- 2 teaspoons cornflour
- 1 tablespoon sugar
- finely sliced spring onions

Clean and scale fish. Trim fins. Scrub cavity of fish well with paper dipped in coarse salt and rinse off excess salt. Dry fish on paper towels, then slash flesh on both sides with shallow parallel cuts from head to tail of fish. Rub grated ginger and teaspoon of salt into slashes and inside cavities.

Heat oil in a wok and fry fish for 3 or 4 minutes on each side, turning once only. Lift out with slotted spoon, letting oil drain into wok, and place fish on warm serving dish. Pour off half the oil in wok and fry garlic and ginger, stirring, over low heat until fragrant and golden. Add chilli bean sauce and soy sauce. Stir well, then add 1 cup water and simmer. Mix cornflour with a little cold water and stir into sauce until it boils and thickens. Add sugar. Pour over fish, sprinkle with spring onions, and serve hot with rice or noodles.

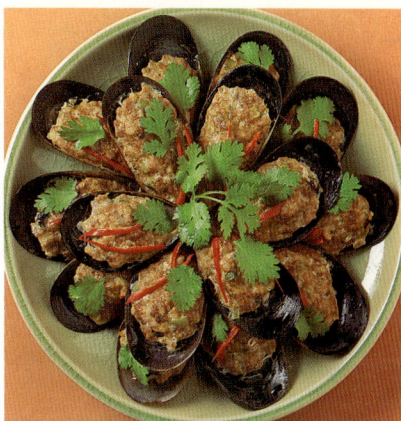

Serve these mussels steamed as a first course or simmer them in a red curry sauce made as in Thai Red Curry of Fish (see p. 3) to serve with steamed rice.

THAI STUFFED MUSSELS
Serves 4

- 500 g (1 lb) mussels
- 185 g (6 oz) minced pork
- 3 teaspoons Thai Red Curry Paste (see p. 80)
- grated rind of ½ lime
- 2 tablespoons finely chopped spring onions
- 2 teaspoons cornflour
- 3 teaspoons fish sauce
- 1 teaspoon palm sugar
- 1 egg white
- red chillies and fresh coriander leaves

Scrub mussels with a stiff brush and beard them by tugging brown fibres near hinge of shell. Discard mussels that are not tightly shut. Place on a rack and steam just until shells open. Remove from heat and remove empty half of shell from each mussel.

Combine pork, Thai Red Curry Paste, rind, spring onions, cornflour, fish sauce, palm sugar and egg white. Spread a teaspoon of mixture over each mussel. Place shreds of chilli and small coriander leaves on each and arrange once again in steamer. Steam for 15 minutes.

This curry is made with live crabs. My method for coping with these nippy monsters is to let them go quietly to sleep in the freezer first, because it is nicer if fresh green crabs are used. Whenever we had this in Sri Lanka, a wooden board and heavy hammer were brought to the table and each diner cracked the claws with a well placed blow while others at the table hid behind their napkins in case of flying curry! Serve only with rice, no other curries or accompaniments, because the flavour is so superb it deserves to be appreciated on its own. Besides, you are so busy picking meat from the crabs there is just no time to concentrate on anything else.

CRAB CURRY
Serves 4 to 6

- 2 large crabs
- 3 medium onions, chopped finely
- 6 cloves garlic, chopped finely
- 2 teaspoons finely grated fresh ginger
- ½ teaspoon fenugreek seeds
- sprig of curry leaves
- 8 cm (3 inch) stick cinnamon
- 1 teaspoon chilli powder
- 1 teaspoon ground turmeric
- 2 teaspoons salt or to taste
- 3½ cups canned coconut milk
- 2 tablespoons desiccated coconut

- 1 tablespoon ground rice
- ¼ cup lime or lemon juice

Remove carapace, the hard top shell, from crabs and discard 'feathers' found underneath. Divide each crab into 4 sections: break each body in half, leaving legs attached, but detach large claws from body.

Put onion, garlic, ginger, fenugreek, curry leaves, cinnamon, chilli, turmeric, salt and 1½ cups of the coconut milk mixed with 2½ cups water into a large saucepan. Cover and simmer gently for 30 minutes. Add crabs. Make sure pieces of crab are submerged in sauce while cooking, otherwise simmer half the pieces at a time.

If using raw crabs cook for 20 minutes, but cooked crabs should be simmered for only 8–10 minutes.

Toast desiccated coconut and ground rice separately in a dry frying pan over medium heat, stirring constantly, until each is golden brown—watch that they don't burn. Transfer to a blender container and add 1 cup of coconut milk. Blend for 1 minute on high speed, then stir into curry with lime or lemon juice. Rinse blender with remaining cup of coconut milk and stir in. Simmer uncovered for 10 minutes more. Serve with plain boiled rice.

POULTRY

Where you shop can determine what certain ingredients are called. To avoid confusion when using this book and buying poultry, here is a short explanation.

Thigh fillets are the thigh meat with skin and bone removed. Thigh cutlets are the thigh joint with skin and bone intact. Chicken thighs are thigh cutlets with a large bit of backbone attached. Chicken soup pieces are usually necks, backs, carcases (with breast fillets removed) and some offcuts of drumsticks if you're lucky. The latter are cheap and ideal for making stock.

To cut chicken into curry pieces means jointing the chicken and then cutting through the joints to make smaller pieces so that spices can penetrate and flavour the meat. A breast should be halved, then each half cut into 3. Thighs and drumsticks should be cut into 2 pieces each. (In Chinese dishes, however, they are cut into 5, not separating them at the joint but chopping either side of the joint and then 2 more cuts on each side. Use a heavy, sharp Chinese cleaver for this sort of chopping through the bone, or you will ruin your best knives.)

Here then is poultry the Asian way—in curries, tangy soups, tantalising stir-fries and spicy braised dishes. There is even a roast that has little in common with the Western roast.

*There are many flavours in this spicy soup, but the predominant
one is galangal, also known as Thai ginger.*

Thai Chicken and Galangal Soup
Serves 6

- 1 kg (2 lb) chicken soup pieces
- 2 cups canned coconut milk
- ½ teaspoon whole black peppercorns
- 6 slices galangal, fresh or in brine
- 3 stems lemon grass, finely sliced
- 4 fresh coriander roots, finely chopped
- 4 fresh green chillies
- 1½ teaspoons salt or to taste
- 6 kaffir lime leaves
- 1–2 tablespoons fish sauce
- ⅓ cup strained lime juice
- ½ cup chopped fresh coriander leaves
- 500 g (1 lb) chicken thighs, skin removed

Put chicken soup pieces in a large saucepan with 2 litres water,
1 cup coconut milk and all ingredients except lime juice,
coriander leaves and chicken thighs. Bring to the boil and
simmer for 1 hour, strain and put thighs in liquid to cook
for a further 35–40 minutes, returning lime leaves and galangal.
Dice chicken meat and return to soup with remaining coconut
milk, lime juice and coriander. Serve hot.

THAI CHICKEN CURRY WITH BASIL
Serves 6

- 500 g (1 lb) chicken thigh cutlets
- 500 g (1 lb) sugar snap peas
3 tablespoons peanut oil
3 tablespoons Thai Red Curry Paste (see p. 80)
- finely grated rind of 1 lime
- 5 kaffir lime leaves
- 2 tablespoons fish sauce
- 1½ cups canned coconut milk
- 1 tablespoon palm sugar
- 20 fresh lemon basil or sweet basil leaves

Cut chicken into bite-size pieces and remove strings from pea pods.

Heat oil in a wok and fry Red Curry Paste over low heat, stirring, until fragrant—about 5 minutes. Add chicken and fry until pieces are coated with paste. Add lime rind, lime leaves, fish sauce, coconut milk plus 1 cup water and simmer for 10 minutes, uncovered.

Drop peas into lightly salted boiling water for 1 minute. Do not overcook. Lift out with slotted spoon and simmer with chicken for a minute or so. Stir in palm sugar. Remove from heat, add basil leaves. Serve with rice.

A meal in one dish.

INDONESIAN CHICKEN SOUP
Serves 6

- 1.5 kg (3 lb) chicken pieces
- 2 teaspoons salt
- 1 teaspoon whole black peppercorns
- a few celery tops
- 1 stalk lemon grass, lightly crushed
- 2 medium onions
- 6 curry leaves
- 2 tablespoons peanut oil
- 3 cloves garlic, chopped finely
- 1 teaspoon finely grated fresh ginger
- ½ teaspoon dried shrimp paste
- ½ teaspoon ground turmeric
- 2 teaspoons ground coriander
- 1 teaspoon ground cummin
- 4 candlenuts or macadamia nuts, grated finely
- 125 g (4 oz) rice vermicelli
- 2 large potatoes, cooked and sliced
- lemon juice to taste
- ½ cup finely sliced spring onions
- 2 hard-boiled eggs, finely chopped
- chopped celery leaves
- 2 tablespoons fried onion flakes

Place chicken pieces in a large saucepan and add sufficient water to cover. Add salt, peppercorns, celery tops, lemon grass and 1 onion, peeled. Bring quickly to the boil, then reduce heat, cover and simmer for about 30 minutes or until chicken is tender. Cool to lukewarm and strain stock into a bowl. Discard skin and bones from chicken. Dice meat and reserve.

Cut remaining onion into slices. Fry onion and curry leaves in peanut oil in saucepan over high heat until golden brown. Add garlic, ginger, shrimp paste, turmeric, coriander, cummin and candlenuts. Fry, stirring, for a few seconds. Add stock, and simmer for 10 minutes. Meanwhile soak rice vermicelli in hot water for 10 minutes, drain and cut into short lengths. Add to soup, boil for 1 minute. Add chicken, potatoes and lemon juice and heat through. Serve garnished with spring onion, egg, celery leaves and fried onion.

COUNTRY CAPTAIN
Serves 4

- *1 roasting chicken*
- *1 teaspoon crushed garlic*
- *1½ teaspoons salt*
- *1½ teaspoons turmeric*
- *½ teaspoon black pepper*
- *¼ cup oil*
- *3 large onions, sliced thinly*
- *2 fresh chillies, sliced*

Cut chicken into joints. Combine garlic and salt to a smooth purée, mix with turmeric and pepper and rub well over chicken. Heat oil and fry two thirds of onion until brown, remove, then fry remaining onion and chillies until onion fragrant. Add chicken and fry until golden. Add ½ cup water, cover and simmer until tender. Uncover and allow liquid to evaporate. Serve hot with reserved fried onion, and fried potatoes or steamed rice.

Hunan-Style Chicken
Serves 4

- 6 large chicken thigh cutlets
- 1 teaspoon Szechwan peppercorns
- ½ teaspoon salt
- 2 tablespoons dark soy sauce
- 2 tablespoons dry sherry
- 2 teaspoons honey
- 3 tablespoons peanut oil
- 3 dried red chillies, cut in pieces
- ¼ cup chopped spring onions
- 1 tablespoon finely chopped ginger
- 2 teaspoons finely chopped garlic
- 2 tablespoons Chinese vinegar
- 1 teaspoon chilli bean sauce
- 1 teaspoon sesame oil

Cut chicken thighs into bite size pieces, chopping through bone. Roast Szechwan peppercorns in a dry pan over low heat for a few minutes, shaking pan or stirring so they don't scorch. Grind to powder in mortar and pestle and sprinkle over chicken pieces with salt. Mix soy sauce, sherry and honey, pour over chicken and mix well.

Heat peanut oil in a wok and fry chillies, spring onions, ginger and garlic until fragrant, stirring constantly. Add chicken and stir-fry on high heat for 2 or 3 minutes, lower heat, cover

17

and simmer until chicken is tender, about 7 minutes.

Combine vinegar, chilli bean sauce and sesame oil and pour over chicken. Toss a few times on high heat. Serve with steamed rice and vegetables.

Chicken Dopiaza
Serves 6

- *1.5 kg (3 lb) chicken pieces*
- *6 medium onions*
- *4 fresh green chillies, seeded*
- *4 cloves garlic, chopped*
- *1 tablespoon finely grated fresh ginger*
- *1 tablespoon each ground coriander and cummin*
- *1 teaspoon each ground cinnamon and cardamom*
- *2 teaspoons ground turmeric*
- *¼ teaspoon ground cloves*
- *3 tablespoons each ghee and oil*
- *3 ripe tomatoes, peeled and chopped*
- *salt to taste*

If using breast halves or thighs, cut across in two. Thinly slice half the onions and set aside. Roughly chop remainder and put into a blender with chillies, garlic and ginger and ground spices. Blend to a purée.

Heat ghee and oil in a large saucepan and fry sliced onions, stirring frequently, until golden brown. Remove from pan with slotted spoon and set aside. Add blended mixture to pan and fry, stirring, until it darkens and oil appears at edges. Stir in tomatoes and cook until liquid is almost evaporated. Add chicken pieces and stir. Add 1 cup water with salt, cover and cook until chicken is tender—about 35 minutes. Stir in reserved onions and simmer 5 minutes more. Serve with rice or parathas.

Braised Mandarin Chicken
Serves 4

- *500 g (1 lb) chicken Maryland*
- *2 mandarins*
- *2 tablespoons dry sherry*
- *2 tablespoons dark soy sauce*
- *2 teaspoons sugar*
- *2 teaspoons green peppercorns in brine*
- *2 tablespoons peanut oil*
- *2 teaspoons finely chopped fresh ginger*
- *3 or 4 dried red chillies, whole*
- *3 or 4 fresh hot chillies, sliced*
- *½ cup spring onions, sliced*
- *1 teaspoon sesame oil*

Cut chicken thighs and drumsticks into 4 or 5 pieces each using a heavy cleaver and chopping straight through bones. Do not separate at joint, but cut on either side of it.

Squeeze juice from 1 mandarin, combine with sherry, soy sauce and sugar. Crush green peppercorns and mix in. Scoop out pith from mandarin halves and cut rind into fine shreds. Wrap in plastic to prevent drying out.

Heat a wok, add peanut oil and when hot fry ginger, dried chillies, fresh chillies and mandarin rind for about 10 seconds. Add chicken pieces and fry on high heat, tossing and pressing against sides of wok, until no longer pink. Add combined liquid ingredients, cover and simmer for 20 to 30 minutes until chicken is tender. Turn pieces in sauce now and then so they are evenly coloured. Meanwhile, peel and segment remaining mandarin.

Add spring onions and cook on high heat, uncovered, until sauce reduces. Sprinkle with sesame oil and garnish with mandarin segments. Serve with steamed rice.

CHICKEN WITH CHILLI RADISH
Serves 4

- *500 g chicken thigh fillets*
- *½ teaspoon salt*
- *½ teaspoon five spice powder*
- *3 tablespoons peanut oil*
- *2 teaspoons finely grated ginger*
- *1 teaspoon finely chopped garlic*
- *2 tablespoons preserved hot radish*
- *2 tablespoons soy sauce*
- *2 tablespoons dry sherry*
- *¼ cup chicken stock*
- *1½ teaspoons cornflour*
- *1 teaspoon sesame oil*

Cut chicken fillets into bite-size squares and rub over with salt and five-spice powder.

Heat oil in a wok and gently fry ginger and garlic for 30 seconds, then add hot radish and fry for a further 10 seconds before adding chicken and stir-frying on high heat until colour changes.

Add soy sauce, sherry and stock and bring to the boil. Cover and simmer for 3 minutes. Mix cornflour with a little cold water and stir into sauce until it boils and thickens. Sprinkle sesame oil over and toss well. Serve with steamed rice.

CHICKEN WITH PEANUT SAUCE
Serves 6

- *1 kg (2 lb) chicken pieces*
- *2 teaspoons crushed garlic*
- *2 teaspoons finely grated ginger*
- *2 tablespoons Thai Red Curry Paste (see p. 80)*
- *3 tablespoons peanut oil*
- *1 cup canned coconut milk*
- *3 tablespoons crunchy peanut butter*
- *2 teaspoons palm sugar*
- *1 small red capsicum, sliced*
- *6 spring onions cut into lengths*

Cut any large pieces of chicken into smaller pieces, e.g. whole breasts can be cut into 6 pieces, drumsticks and thighs into 2, wings just have the tips removed. Rub all over with garlic, ginger and 2 teaspoons of Thai Red Curry Paste. Cover and set aside 30 minutes.

Heat oil in a wok and fry chicken pieces until lightly browned. Remove from wok and on low heat fry remaining curry paste, stirring, until fragrant. Add coconut milk and 1 cup water and simmer 10 minutes. Return chicken to wok, cover and simmer until chicken is tender. Stir in peanut butter and palm sugar, capsicum and spring onions and cook for 5 minutes longer. Serve with rice.

In this western province of India, this combination of spices is popular—not only for chicken but for seafood as well. Each spice is roasted separately because of their varying sizes. If they are all put into the pan together the larger seeds will not be roasted enough, while small seeds may be overdone.

CHICKEN MAHARASHTRA
Serves 6

- 1 x 1.5 kg (3 lb) chicken pieces
- 5 large dried red chillies
- 1 tablespoon each coriander and white poppy seeds
- 1 teaspoon cummin seeds
- ¼ teaspoon black peppercorns
- 1 cup fresh grated coconut or ½ cup desiccated coconut
- 2 medium onions, sliced finely
- 1 teaspoon ground turmeric
- ½ teaspoon each ground cloves and cardamom
- 1 tablespoon ghee or butter
- 2 tablespoons oil
- 2 cloves garlic, chopped
- 1 teaspoon chopped ginger
- salt to taste
- 1 small stick cinnamon
- juice of 1 lime

If using breasts halves or thighs, cut across in two. Set aside. Soak chillies in hot water for 10 minutes. Meanwhile roast separately coriander, poppy seeds, cummin, black peppercorns and coconut in a small dry pan over medium heat, stirring constantly, for about 2 minutes or until colour changes and they become fragrant. Turn each out onto a plate. Add sliced onion to pan and dry roast, stirring, until lightly browned.

Transfer chillies to a blender with a little of the soaking water; add all roasted ingredients and turmeric, cloves and cardamom. Grind to a paste. Heat ghee and oil in a large, heavy pan and fry ground mixture with garlic and ginger, stirring constantly, until oil separates. Add chicken and stir until coated. Add salt and ½ cup water and bring to a gentle simmer. Cover and cook over very low heat, stirring occasionally, until chicken is tender. Add more water as necessary. Sauce should be dark and very thick. Stir in lime juice. Serve with rice and pickles.

Serve with rice or as an exciting filling for sandwiches.

INDONESIAN EGG SAMBAL
Serves 4 to 6

- *4 eggs*
- *3 tablespoons peanut oil*
- *1 onion, finely chopped*
- *1 teaspoon crushed garlic*
- *½ teaspoon dried shrimp paste*
- *1 tablespoon sambal ulek or chopped red chillies*
- *1 teaspoon finely chopped galangal, fresh or bottled*
- *6 candlenuts or macadamias, finely grated or pounded*
- *2 teaspoons palm sugar*
- *½ cup canned coconut milk*
- *salt to taste*
- *2 tablespoons lime or lemon juice*

Have eggs at room temperature or gently warm them in tepid water before cooking them. Stir for the first few minutes so yolks are centred, then simmer for 8 minutes. Cool in a bowl of cold water. Shell eggs and halve lengthways.

Heat oil and fry onion and garlic until onion is soft and golden. Add shrimp paste, sambal, galangal and candlenuts and fry, stirring, until fragrant. Add palm sugar, coconut milk, salt and lime juice and simmer, stirring frequently, until oil shines on surface. Put in eggs, spooning sauce over.

Sri Lanka Chicken Curry
Serves 4 to 6

- 3 tablespoons ghee or oil
- 10 curry leaves
- 2 large onions, chopped finely
- 5 cloves garlic, chopped finely
- 2 teaspoons finely grated fresh ginger
- 2 tablespoons Ceylon Curry Powder (see p. 79)
- 2 teaspoons salt
- 2 tablespoons vinegar
- 1.5 kg (3 lb) roasting chicken, jointed
- 2 ripe tomatoes, peeled and chopped
- 6 cardamom pods, bruised
- 1 stick cinnamon
- 1 stalk lemon grass, bruised
- 1 cup canned coconut milk

Heat ghee and fry curry leaves until they start to brown. Add onions, garlic and ginger and fry over low heat until onions are soft and golden, stirring frequently. Stir in Ceylon Curry Powder, salt and vinegar. Add chicken pieces and cook over medium heat, turning until thoroughly coated. Add tomatoes, whole spices and lemon grass and cook, covered, over low heat for 40 minutes or until tender. Stir in coconut milk and heat through. Serve with rice and accompaniments.

Chicken Satay
Serves 6

- 750 g (1½ lb) chicken thigh fillets
1 tablespoon Green Masala Paste (see p. 84)

Cut chicken into bite-size pieces, marinade in paste for 30 minutes. Thread on skewers and grill until done. Serve with Peanut Sauce, (see p. 75) and sliced onions, tomatoes, cucumbers.

*I won't make you count out 100 almonds for this rich North Indian
curry—the number translates into 125 g (4 oz), or ⅔ cup.*

One-Hundred Almond Curry
Serves 6

- *1.5 kg (3 lb) chicken pieces*
- *4 large onions*
- *¼ cup ghee or oil*
- *1 tablespoon each finely chopped garlic and ginger*
- *1 tablespoon each ground coriander and cummin*
- *1 teaspoon each ground chilli and turmeric*
- *½ teaspoon ground fennel*
- *salt to taste*
- *3 large ripe tomatoes, peeled and chopped*
- *¼ cup chopped fresh mint leaves*
- *1 cup plain yoghurt*
- *125 g (4 oz) whole blanched almonds, toasted*
- *1 teaspoon Garam Masala (see p. 78)*

If chicken pieces are large, cut across into halves with a sharp
cleaver. Finely chop 3 of the onions and cut the fourth into
fine slices. Heat ghee in a large, heavy saucepan and fry sliced
onion, stirring, until golden brown. Remove from pan and set
aside. Add chopped onion, garlic and ginger to ghee left in
pan and fry over low heat, stirring occasionally, until soft and
turning golden. Make sure that onions are cooked very slowly.

Add coriander, cummin, chilli, turmeric and fennel and fry, stirring, for 1 to 2 minutes. Stir in salt, tomatoes and half the mint; cook, covered, until tomatoes are pulpy. Stir occasionally so that mixture does not stick to base of pan.

Add chicken pieces and stir to coat with mixture. Cover and cook very gently for 40 minutes, or until chicken is tender. Beat yoghurt until smooth and stir into curry with half the almonds. Simmer 5 minutes, uncovered. Grind remaining almonds in a blender and add to curry with remaining mint and Garam Masala. Heat through and serve.

CURRIED CHICKEN LIVERS
Serves 4 to 6

- 500 g (1 lb) chicken livers, washed and trimmed
- 2 tablespoons ghee
- 2 medium onions, chopped finely
- 1 clove garlic, crushed
- 2 teaspoons finely grated fresh ginger
- ½ teaspoon each ground turmeric and chilli powder
- 1 tablespoon ground coriander
- 1 teaspoon each ground cummin and fennel
- 2 ripe tomatoes, peeled and chopped
- salt to taste
- 1 teaspoon Fragrant Garam Masala (see p. 78)

Slice livers into halves. Heat ghee in a heavy saucepan and fry onions, stirring occasionally, until soft. Add garlic and ginger and fry, stirring, until golden. Add turmeric, chilli powder, coriander, cummin and fennel and fry, stirring, for 2 minutes. Stir in tomatoes and salt and cook gently, covered, until tomatoes are puréed. Stir occasionally. Add chicken livers and stir. Cover and cook for 15 minutes. Sprinkle with Fragrant Garam Masala and simmer for 2 minutes more. Serve hot with rice and accompaniments.

Sataw nuts are the seeds of a giant bean, popular in southern Thailand. Their flavour and smell are definitely an acquired taste— only for the adventurous curry buffs! In Malaysia and Indonesia they are called petai *or* peteh. *Purchase them in cans or jars.*

GREEN CURRY OF DUCK WITH SATAW NUTS
Serves 6

- *1 x 2kg (4 lb) roasting duck*
- *1 x 400 mL (14 fl oz) can coconut milk*
- *3 tablespoons Thai Green Curry Paste (see p. 81)*
- *6 kaffir lime leaves*
- *2 tablespoons fish sauce*
- *½ cup drained sataw nuts*
- *salt to taste*
- *4–6 fresh green chillies, seeded and chopped*
- *½ cup chopped fresh basil leaves*

Cut duck into joints. Take ¾ cup of rich coconut milk and heat in a wok or heavy saucepan until thick and oily. Add Green Curry Paste and cook over low heat, stirring, 3 or 4 minutes or until fragrant and oily on surface. Add duck and remaining coconut milk mixed with 2 cups water.

Add lime leaves and fish sauce, stir well, cover and simmer for 1½ hours or until duck is almost tender. Add sataw nuts and salt to taste and simmer for a further 15 minutes. Just before serving stir in chillies and basil. Serve with rice.

Giving leftovers a new image after the Christmas feast may not sound particularly Asian, but happens in many countries which have been converted to Christianity or colonised by the British. They therefore celebrate Christmas with the traditional fare. Try this spicy treatment of cold turkey.

DEVILLED TURKEY
Serves 6

- 500 g (1 lb) cold, cooked turkey
- 2 teaspoons crushed garlic
- 1 teaspoon salt
- 1 teaspoon finely grated fresh ginger
- 1 tablespoon vinegar
- 1 tablespoon Worcestershire Sauce
- 1 or 2 tablespoons chilli sauce
- 2 tablespoons arrack, or whisky
- 2 teaspoons prepared grain mustard
- 2 teaspoons sugar
- 1 teaspoon freshly ground pepper
- 2 tablespoons dripping from roast, or ghee
- 2 large onions cut in thick slices
- 2 sprigs fresh curry leaves, or about 20 dried leaves
- strips of pandan leaf
- 1 stem lemon grass
- 2 cups turkey stock
- 4 whole cloves
- small stick of cinnamon
- 500 g (1 lb) potatoes, peeled and sliced

Cut turkey into joints or slices. Crush garlic with salt and mix with ginger, vinegar, Worcestershire Sauce, chilli sauce, arrack, mustard, sugar and pepper. Marinade turkey in mixture for 30 minutes.

Heat dripping in a heavy saucepan and fry onions, curry leaves, pandan leaf and lemon grass until onions are deep brown. Add marinated turkey, stock, cloves and cinnamon, cover and simmer for 15 minutes. Add potatoes, cover and cook until done. Serve hot.

This is cheating, but I'm quite prepared to do it when it cuts the usual cooking time of duck by more than 1 hour and gives such tender, delicious results.

QUICK BARBECUE STYLE DUCK
Serves 4 to 5

- *1 x 2 kg (4 lb) roasting duck*
- *2 cloves garlic, crushed*
- *2 teaspoons finely grated fresh ginger*
- *2 tablespoons hoi sin sauce*
- *2 tablespoons honey*
- *2 tablespoons dark soy sauce*
- *3 teaspoons smooth peanut butter*
- *2 teaspoons oriental sesame oil*
- *spring onion brushes (see Note)*
- *plum sauce*

Wash duck inside and out and dry with paper towels. Mix remaining ingredients, except spring onion brushes and plum sauce, in a small pan, heating gently and stirring until smooth. If mixture seems too thick add a teaspoon or two of water.

Rub enough mixture inside and outside duck to cover all surfaces, and reserve the rest to serve as sauce. Marinate duck for 1 hour. Put duck in oven bag and make a few holes in bag near the tie. Microwave at 70% power for 35 minutes or place in a roasting dish and cook in a moderate oven (180°C,

350°F) for 1 hour. Remove from bag, carve and serve hot with reserved marinade, Mandarin Pancakes (see below), spring onion brushes and plum sauce. Each person paints a pancake with marinade or sauce using a spring onion brush, puts a slice of duck and onion in centre, rolls up pancake and eats it. If you can do it all with chopsticks, you get the Peking Duck Award!

Note   To make spring onion brushes, cut into 7 cm (2¾ inch) lengths and with a sharp pointed knife slit one end of spring onion several times. Drop into a bowl of iced water to curl.

MANDARIN PANCAKES
Makes 20

- *2 cups plain (all-purpose) flour*
- *¾ cup boiling water*
- *1 tablespoon oriental sesame oil*

Put unsifted flour into a large bowl and pour boiling water onto flour, stirring with chopsticks. When cool enough to handle, knead for 10 minutes or until smooth. Cover and leave for 30 minutes.

Shape dough into a long roll and cut into 10 equal slices. Keep covered with plastic so surface does not become dry. Take one slice, divide in halves and roll each to a smooth ball between palms. With a lightly floured rolling pin, roll to two circles about 8 cm (3 inches) in diameter. Brush one with sesame oil, place second circle on top and roll out both circles together, until 15 cm (6 inches) across and very thin. Cover with greaseproof.

Heat a heavy frying pan and cook on low heat until pancake blisters. Turn frequently so both sides cook evenly. When a few golden spots show, pancake is done. It should be soft and pliable. Gently pull the two circles apart (this is easy due to the sesame oil), fold in quarters and keep covered. May be made a day ahead and warmed by steaming gently.

Duck, being a rich and fatty meat, is improved by being cooked in a dish like Vindaloo with its high acid content to offset the richness.

Duck Vindaloo
Serves 4 to 5

- 1 x 2.5 kg (5 lb) duck
- 8 large dried red chillies
- ¾ cup white wine vinegar
- 4 cloves garlic, chopped
- 1 tablespoon chopped fresh ginger
- 1 tablespoon ground coriander
- 2 teaspoons ground cummin
- 1 teaspoon Fragrant Garam Masala (see p. 78)
- ½ teaspoon ground black pepper
- 2 tablespoons oil
- salt to taste
- 1 tablespoon brown sugar

Cut duck into joints. Remove and discard stalks and seeds from chillies and soak in vinegar for 10 minutes. Put chillies, vinegar, garlic and ginger into a blender and process until smooth. Transfer mixture to a large bowl and mix in ground spices. Add duck pieces and turn until well coated. Cover and leave for 2 hours, or refrigerate overnight.

Heat oil in a large non-aluminium saucepan and lightly fry duck pieces. Mix in salt and a little hot water with remaining marinade. Cover and simmer gently until duck is tender. Add a little more water if necessary during cooking. Stir in sugar when duck is cooked. Serve with rice.

This is an Asian version of duck stew–with a spicy difference.

DUCK WITH POTATOES AND ONIONS
Serves 4 to 5

- *1 x 2 kg (4 lb) duck*
- *1 clove garlic, crushed*
- *1 teaspoon finely grated fresh ginger*
- *1 teaspoon each ground turmeric and black pepper*
- *3 tablespoons oil*
- *12 tiny onions, peeled and left whole*
- *12 small new potatoes, scrubbed*
- *2 large onions, chopped finely*
- *1 teaspoon chilli powder, optional*
- *4 fresh green chillies, seeded and sliced*
- *2 small sticks cinnamon*
- *½ teaspoon whole cloves*
- *1 teaspoon cardamon pods, bruised*
- *salt to taste*
- *½ cup white wine vinegar*
- *1 tablespoon Green Masala Paste (see p. 84)*
- *1 tablespoon brown sugar*

Cut duck into joints. Mix garlic, ginger, turmeric and black pepper and rub over joints. Set aside for 1 hour. Heat oil in a large stainless steel or enamel saucepan and lightly brown whole onions and potatoes. Remove from pan and set aside. Add chopped onions to pan and fry, stirring, until soft and golden. Stir in chilli powder, then add duck and brown. Add green chillies, whole spices, salt and vinegar. Stir in 3 cups water, cover and simmer gently for 2 hours or until duck is almost tender, adding extra hot water if necessary. Add reserved onions and potatoes and Green Masala Paste for last 30 minutes of cooking time. Stir in sugar when duck is cooked. Serve with rice.

MEAT

Because of their long, slow cooking time, curries are ideal for budget cuts of meat as they improve the flavour while tenderising the meat. Of course, not every spiced dish is a curry and you will also find some stir-fried dishes, a spicy Thai salad and a meltingly tender steamed pork dish in the Chinese tradition.

FRIKKADELS
Makes 30 to 40

- 1 onion, finely chopped
- 2 cloves garlic, crushed
- 30 g (1 oz) butter
- 500 g (1 lb) minced beef
- ½ cup soft breadcrumbs
- 1 teaspoon salt
- ½ teaspoon ground black pepper
- 1 teaspoon Garam Masala (see p. 78)
- 3 teaspoons chopped fresh dill
- 3 teaspoons Worcestershire sauce
- 1 egg, beaten
- dry breadcrumbs for coating
- oil or ghee for frying

Gently fry onion and garlic in butter until golden. Combine thoroughly with all the ingredients except last three. Form into small balls about 2.5 cm (1 inch) in diameter, dip in beaten egg and roll in dry breadcrumbs to coat. Deep fry in oil or ghee until golden brown all over, drain on paper towels and serve hot.

A great favourite because there is so much flavour incorporated into the meatballs. At times when you need to budget, it's an unfailing way to make economy-priced minced steak taste even better than expensive T-bone or fillet steak.

PUNJABI MEATBALL CURRY
Serves 6

MEATBALLS
- 750 g (1½ lb) finely minced lamb
- 1 medium onion, finely chopped
- 1 teaspoon crushed garlic
- 1 teaspoon finely grated fresh ginger
- 1 fresh red chilli, seeded and chopped finely
- ¼ cup chopped fresh coriander leaves
- 1 teaspoon salt or to taste
- 1 teaspoon ground coriander
- 1 teaspoon Garam Masala (see p. 78)

SAUCE
2 tablespoons ghee
- 2 medium onions, chopped finely
- 2 teaspoons finely chopped garlic
- 1 tablespoon finely chopped fresh ginger
- 1 teaspoon ground turmeric
- 1 teaspoon chilli powder or to taste
- 1 teaspoon Garam Masala (see p. 78)
- 2 ripe tomatoes, peeled and chopped
- salt to taste
- 2 tablespoons chopped fresh mint leaves
- lime or lemon juice to taste

MEATBALLS   Mix all ingredients together and shape into small balls. Brown meatballs, remove from pan and set aside.

SAUCE   Heat ghee in a large, heavy saucepan. Add onions, garlic and ginger and fry until soft and golden. Stir in turmeric, chilli and Garam Masala and fry for 1 minute. Add meatballs with tomatoes and salt; cover and simmer for 25 minutes or until meatballs are cooked and sauce has thickened. Stir in mint and lime juice and serve with rice or chapatis.

Typical of Kashmiri food, this curry has a rich red sauce with the fragrance of saffron.

LAMB KOFTAS IN SAFFRON SAUCE
Serves 6

- *750 g (1½ lb) boneless lamb*
- *1 ½ teaspoons Garam Masala (see p. 78)*
- *1 teaspoon salt*
- *3 tablespoons arrowroot*
- *1 teaspoon turmeric*
- *1 or 2 teaspoons chilli powder, to taste*
- *2 tablespoons ghee or oil*
- *1 medium onion, sliced finely*
- *2 teaspoons finely chopped fresh ginger*
- *1 small stick cinnamon*
- *4 whole cloves*
- *3 cardamom pods, bruised*
- *2 teaspoons each paprika and tomato paste*
- *¼ teaspoon saffron strands*
- *2 tablespoons finely chopped coriander leaves*

Chop meat roughly into cubes and process in a food processor, a quarter at a time, until a smooth paste. Mix Garam Masala, salt and arrowroot with 2 tablespoons cold water until smooth. Add to meat. Form into ovals the size of an egg. Poach in a saucepan with 5 cm (2 inches) lightly salted boiling water, half the turmeric and chilli powder for 10 minutes.

Heat ghee or oil and fry onion, ginger and whole spices until onion is soft and golden. Stir in remaining turmeric and chilli powder with paprika and tomato paste. Add meat balls with some of their cooking liquid. Cover and simmer until tender—about 30 minutes. Lightly toast saffron strands in a dry pan, crush to powder and dissolve in 2 tablespoons boiling water. Stir in towards end of cooking and garnish with coriander leaves. Serve with rice and vegetables.

LIVER CURRY
Serves 4

- *3 tablespoons oil*
- *8 curry leaves*
- *2 medium onions, chopped finely*
- *2 cloves garlic, chopped finely*
- *2 teaspoons finely chopped fresh ginger*
- *2 fresh chillies, seeded and chopped*
- *1 tablespoon ground coriander*
- *1 teaspoon each ground cummin and chilli powder*
- *½ teaspoon ground turmeric*
- *500 g (1 lb) diced lamb or calf liver*
- *1 tablespoon Green Masala Paste (see p. 84)*
- *¾ cup canned coconut milk*
- *salt to taste*
- *2 tablespoons lime or lemon juice*

Heat oil in a heavy saucepan and fry curry leaves, onions, garlic, ginger and chillies over medium heat, stirring frequently, until onions are golden brown. Stir in coriander, cummin, chilli powder and turmeric and fry, stirring constantly, for 1 minute. Add liver and toss until colour changes. Stir in Green Masala Paste, coconut milk and salt mixed with ¾ cup water. Simmer, uncovered, until liver is tender and sauce has thickened. Stir in lime juice and serve with rice.

Meat and Potato Curry
Serves 6 to 8

- *1.5 kg (3 lb) lean lamb*
- *¼ cup oil*
- *1 tablespoon Whole Spice Mix (see p. 77)*
- *2 large onions, sliced finely*
- *6 cloves garlic, chopped*
- *1 tablespoon finely chopped ginger*
- *1 teaspoon ground turmeric*
- *2 tablespoons ground coriander*
- *2 teaspoons chilli powder*
- *2 teaspoons salt or to taste*
- *¼ cup vinegar*
- *2 teaspoons Garam Masala (see p. 78)*
- *750 g (1½ lb) potatoes, peeled and cubed*
- *2 tablespoons chopped fresh mint leaves*

Cut lamb into small cubes. Heat oil in a large, heavy saucepan and fry Whole Spice Mix until mustard seeds pop. Add onions, garlic and ginger and fry over medium heat, stirring occasionally, just until onions begin to brown.

Stir in turmeric and fry 1 minute more. Add coriander and chilli powder, stir, then add salt and half the vinegar, stirring until liquid evaporates. Sprinkle in Garam Masala, add cubed lamb and stir until all pieces are coated with spice mixture. Add remaining vinegar and scrape up any mixture sticking to base of pan. Lower heat, cover pan tightly and simmer until lamb is almost tender. Add a little water during cooking if necessary.

Add potatoes and cook, covered, for a further 20 to 25 minutes, or until tender. Serve sprinkled with mint leaves and accompanied by rice or Indian bread.

CURRIED FOREQUARTER CHOPS
Serves 6 to 8

- *1.5 kg (3 lb) lamb forequarter chops*
- *3 tablespoons oil*
- *2 large onions, chopped finely*
- *1 tablespoon each finely chopped garlic and ginger*
- *8 cardamom pods, bruised*
- *3 teaspoons each ground coriander and cummin*
- *1 teaspoon ground fennel*
- *½ teaspoon each ground black pepper and chilli*
- *¼ cup ground almonds*
- *2 cups canned tomatoes*
- *1 cup plain yoghurt, beaten until smooth*
- *salt to taste*
- *1 tablespoon lime or lemon juice*
- *¼ cup chopped coriander leaves*

Ask butcher to saw chops across into 2 or 3 pieces.

Heat oil in a large saucepan and fry onions, garlic, ginger and cardamom pods, stirring frequently, until onions are soft and golden. Stir in ground spices and almonds and fry 1 minute more, then add tomatoes and stir well. Cover and simmer until tomatoes are pulpy. Add yoghurt and salt.

Add meat, turning until pieces are coated with sauce. Cover and cook until meat is tender and sauce thick and dark. (Add a little water if mixture sticks to base of pan.) Stir in lime juice and garnish with fresh coriander. Serve with rice or chapatis.

Chilli Beef with Snow Peas
Serves 4

- 375 g (12 oz) lean rump or fillet steak
- 1 teaspoon crushed garlic
- 1 tablespoon soy sauce
- 2 teaspoons chilli bean sauce
- 100 g (3½ oz) snow peas
- 6 spring onions
- 2 large red chillies
- 2 tablespoons peanut oil
- ½ cup beef stock
- 2 teaspoons cornflour
- 2 tablespoons Chinese wine or dry sherry
- 1 teaspoon sesame oil

Freeze beef just until firm enough to cut into paper thin slices. Rub with a mixture of garlic, soy sauce and chilli bean sauce.

String snow peas and if large, cut in halves. Cut spring onions into bite-size lengths. Seed and slice chillies.

Heat a wok, add oil and when oil is hot, add beef and stir-fry over high heat until meat is no longer pink. Add snow peas, onions, chillies and stir-fry a further minute. Add stock and bring to the boil, then stir in cornflour mixed with a tablespoon of cold water and stir until sauce clears and thickens. Add wine and sesame oil, give a quick toss through and serve at once with steamed rice.

Lamb Curry
Serves 6

- 1 kg (2 lb) lean, boneless lamb
- 6 green chillies, seeded and chopped roughly
- ¼ cup coriander leaves
- 1 tablespoon chopped garlic
- 1 tablespoon chopped fresh ginger
- 1 teaspoon ground turmeric
- 4 large onions
- 3 tablespoons ghee or oil
- salt to taste
- 2 tablespoons desiccated coconut
- 1 teaspoon fennel seeds
- 1 tablespoon each ground coriander and cummin
- 1 cup peeled and chopped tomatoes
- 1 cup peeled and cubed potatoes
- ½ cup canned coconut milk

Cut lamb into cubes and place in a bowl. Grind chillies, coriander leaves, garlic, ginger and turmeric to a paste in a food processor or blender, adding a little water. Mix with meat and leave to marinate for 2 hours or overnight in refrigerator.

Cut 1 onion into fairly thick slices and separate into rings. Finely chop remaining onions. Heat ghee or oil in a large, heavy saucepan and fry onion rings until they begin to brown. Remove from pan with slotted spoon and drain on paper towel. Add chopped onions to pan and fry, stirring frequently, until golden. Add meat and fry over high heat, tossing, until browned. Stir in 1 cup water and salt and simmer, covered, for 30 minutes.

Roast coconut and fennel seeds separately in a dry pan. Crush and stir into pan with coriander, cummin and tomatoes. Cover and cook for 20 minutes. Add potatoes with a little water if necessary and continue cooking until potatoes are tender—about 20 minutes. Mix coconut milk with ½ cup water and stir into pan. Cook, uncovered, for 10 minutes more. Serve hot, garnished with onion rings and accompanied by rice or chapatis.

A popular dish throughout South East Asia. Ideal for barbecues.

SPICY SATAY WITH PEANUT SAUCE
Serves 6

- 750 g (1½ lb) tender, lean pork or beef
- 1 large onion
- 2 cloves garlic
- 2 tablespoons light soy sauce
- 1 stem finely sliced lemon grass or grated rind of 1 lemon
- 3 teaspoons ground coriander
- 2 teaspoons ground cummin
- 1 teaspoon ground turmeric
- ½ teaspoon ground fennel
- 1 teaspoon salt
- 1 teaspoon sugar
- Peanut Sauce (see p. 75)

Cut meat into small cubes. In food processor or blender purée onion, garlic, soy sauce and lemon grass or rind. Add remaining ingredients and blend again, then pour over meat, mix well to ensure all pieces are coated with marinade and leave for 1 hour or longer in refrigerator. Meanwhile, soak bamboo skewers in cold water so they will not burn readily.

Thread 5 or 6 pieces of meat on each skewer, leaving half bare. Wrap bare end in foil. Grill over barbecue or under a hot grill until brown. Serve with Peanut Sauce.

One of my favourite curries, not only for its superb flavour, but for its easy preparation. A word of advice—although galangal is used in small amounts, its flavour is vital to the authenticity of rendang—Indonesia's most popular beef dish.

INDONESIAN BEEF CURRY
Serves 8

- 1.5 kg (3 lb) lean stewing beef
- 3 large onions
- 4 large cloves garlic
- 1 tablespoon chopped fresh ginger
- 6–8 fresh red chillies
  or 1 tablespoon sambal ulek
- 1 stem fresh lemon grass, thinly sliced or grated rind of 1 lemon
- 2 teaspoons chopped greater galangal (laos)
- 1 teaspoon chopped lesser galangal (kencur)
  or ½ teaspoon dried ground kencur
- 1 tablespoon ground coriander
- 1 teaspoon ground cummin
- 1 teaspoon ground black pepper
- 2½ cups canned coconut milk
- 1 tablespoon dried tamarind
- salt to taste
- 2 teaspoons palm or brown sugar

Cut beef into large cubes. Roughly chop onions and purée in a blender or food processor with garlic, ginger, chillies or sambal ulek, lemon grass or rind, galangal and ground spices.

Put beef into a large saucepan with 1½ cups coconut milk mixed with 1½ cups water and puréed mixture. Bring to the boil, stirring. Soak tamarind in ½ cup hot water, squeeze to dissolve pulp, and strain. Add tamarind liquid and about 2 teaspoons salt, reduce heat and simmer, uncovered, until meat is tender and liquid has almost evaporated.

Add remaining coconut milk and the palm sugar, stirring constantly. Simmer again until gravy is very thick and reduced to a small amount. Serve with steamed rice and a vegetable sayur made as for Bean Sayur (see p. 54).

Don't be daunted by the large amounts of garlic and ginger in this Burmese curry—they are essential to its wonderful flavour.

Burmese Pork Curry

Serves 8 to 10

- *2 kg (4 lb) pork*
- *4 medium onions, chopped roughly*
- *20 cloves garlic*
- *1 cup peeled and roughly chopped fresh ginger*
- *1 stem lemon grass or 3 strips lemon rind, finely chopped*
- *2 teaspoons salt*
- *2 tablespoons vinegar*
- *2 teaspoons chilli powder*
- *¾ cup peanut oil*
- *¼ cup sesame oil*
- *1 teaspoon ground turmeric*

Cut pork into 2.5 cm (1 inch) cubes. Purée onions, garlic, ginger and lemon grass in a food processor or blender. Transfer to a stainless steel strainer set over a bowl.

With back of a spoon, push mixture to extract as much liquid as possible. Reserve solids and pour liquid into a large saucepan. Add pork, salt, vinegar, chilli and half the peanut oil. Bring to the boil, then reduce heat, cover and simmer gently for 1 to 1½ hours or until pork is almost tender, adding a little hot water if necessary.

In another large pan with heavy base, heat remaining peanut oil and sesame oil until very hot. Carefully add solids left in strainer—they will sputter. Stir in turmeric. Turn heat low and cook covered, but lift lid frequently to stir and scrape base of pan with a wooden spoon. If mixture fries too quickly and begins to stick before onions are transparent, stir in a little water from time to time. It is ready when ingredients have turned a rich red-brown colour, smell cooked, and oil has separated from mass—about 25 minutes.

Add contents of first saucepan to cooked onion mixture, stir and cook, uncovered, until the oil separates once more and liquid has almost evaporated. Stir frequently to make sure mixture does not stick to base of pan. Serve with steamed rice and cooked vegetables or cucumber relish.

Burmese Cucumber Relish
Serves 6

- *2 large green cucumbers*
- *½ cup vinegar*
- *1 teaspoon salt*
- *2 tablespoons peanut oil*
- *2 tablespoons oriental sesame oil*
- *2 tablespoons dried garlic slices*
- *2 tablespoons dried onion flakes*
- *2 tablespoons toasted sesame seeds*

Peel cucumbers, scoop out seeds and cut into strips, then into 5 cm (2 inch) lengths. Put 2 cups water into a non-aluminium saucepan, add vinegar and salt and bring to the boil. Add cucumbers and cook until they begin to look transparent. Drain immediately and cool.

Heat both oils, fry garlic and onion on low heat, drain and cool. Dress cucumber with the oil, sprinkle with garlic, onion and sesame seeds and toss lightly.

Often made with one large piece of beef. Some cooks, however, cut the meat into large pieces about the size of a fillet steak.

Beef Smoore
Serves 6

- 1.5 kg (3 lb) blade or round stewing steak
- 2 large onions, finely chopped
- 2 teaspoons finely chopped garlic
- 1 tablespoon finely chopped fresh ginger
- 2 small sticks cinnamon
- 3 sprigs fresh curry leaves
- 2 stems lemon grass or finely peeled rind 1 lemon
- 3 tablespoons Ceylon Curry Powder (see p. 79)
- ½ teaspoon fenugreek seeds
- ½ cup malt vinegar
- 1 pickled lime or lemon (see Note)
- 2 teaspoons dried tamarind pulp dissolved in ½ cup hot water
- 1 teaspoon turmeric
- 2 teaspoons chilli powder or to taste
- 2 teaspoons salt or to taste
- 1½ cups canned coconut milk
- 2 tablespoons ghee
- 2 tablespoons oil

If using beef in one piece, pierce several times with a metal skewer so flavours penetrate. Put into a large, heavy pan with all ingredients except coconut milk, ghee and oil. Add 1 cup coconut milk and 1½ cups water, cover and simmer until meat is tender—about 2 hours.

If using individual slices of beef, simmer gravy first for 1 hour, then add meat and simmer until tender. Add remaining ½ cup coconut milk and cook, uncovered, a further 15 minutes. Remove from heat, lift out beef and in a frying pan heat ghee and oil and brown meat on all sides. Return to sauce, heat through and serve with rice and accompaniments.

Note   In a large glass jar put layers of quartered limes or lemons and coarse salt. Cover with non-metal lid and leave for at least 6 months by which time fruit will be brown and juices jellied. In the meantime, use ¼ cup extra vinegar.

If you like spicy food that's quick to cook, this Asian version of schnitzel is sure to please.

Spicy Schnitzel
Serves 4

- *4 schnitzels or minute steaks*
- *salt and freshly ground black pepper*
- *ground cloves*
- *2 tablespoons finely chopped onion*
- *2 teaspoons chopped dill weed*
- *1 large egg, beaten*
- *dry breadcrumbs for coating*
- *ghee or oil for frying*

Place steaks on wooden board and season both sides of each steak liberally with freshly ground black pepper, salt and cloves. Mix onion and dill and sprinkle over. With meat mallet or base of a stout bottle, pound onions and dill into steaks. Dip in beaten egg, then in breadcrumbs, pressing them on well. Fry in hot ghee or oil until golden brown and serve at once.

SPICY SPARERIBS
Serves 6 to 8

- *2.5 kg (5 lb) lean, American-style pork spareribs*
- *4 large cloves garlic, peeled*
- *1 teaspoon sugar*
- *1 teaspoon salt*
- *½ teaspoon five spice powder*
- *½ teaspoon white pepper*
- *½ teaspoon chilli powder*
- *¼ cup light soy sauce*
- *2 tablespoons peanut oil*
- *3 tablespoons tomato sauce*
- *1 tablespoon honey*

Ask butcher to cut ribs into short lengths and separate them into groups of 3 or 4 ribs. Crush garlic with sugar and salt, mix with five spice powder, pepper, chilli powder and soy sauce. Pour over ribs, rubbing well. Marinate for 1 hour.

In a large, heavy frying pan heat peanut oil and brown ribs in batches. Add tomato sauce, honey and ½ cup hot water stirred together until honey dissolves. Cover and simmer until tender, then spoon sauce over and cook uncovered until ribs are nicely glazed. (If you like, finish ribs over a barbecue.) Serve with steamed rice and a bottled sauce, such as sweet chilli sauce or plum sauce.

*A specialty of Goa on the west coast of India. Reduce chillies if
a hot curry is not to your taste.*

PORK AND LIVER CURRY
Serves 6 to 8

- *750 g (1 ½ lb) boneless pork*
- *250 g (8 oz) calf's liver*
- *12 large, dried red chillies*
- *1 cup white wine vinegar*
- *3 fresh green chillies, chopped roughly*
- *2 tablespoons each chopped fresh ginger and garlic*
- *2 teaspoons each ground coriander and cummin*
- *1 teaspoon each ground turmeric and cinnamon*
- *½ teaspoon each ground cloves and black pepper*
- *1½ teaspoons salt or to taste*
- *1 tablespoon dried tamarind pulp*
- *1 teaspoon brown sugar*

Place pork in a saucepan with just enough lightly salted water
to cover. Bring to boil and simmer gently for 5 minutes. Reserve
pork stock and cut pork, including skin and fat, into large
dice. Repeat with liver, but discard cooking liquid. Let liver
cool and dice finely.

Discard stalks and seeds from dried chillies, soak chillies
in vinegar for 10 minutes, then blend chillies, vinegar, green
chillies, ginger and garlic to a purée. Add ground spices and
salt.

In a non-aluminium saucepan put pork with stock, liver
and spice mixture. Cover and simmer about 1 hour or until
pork is tender. Dissolve tamarind in ½ cup hot water, strain
and add with sugar to pan. Continue cooking, uncovered, until
sauce is thick and dark. Serve with plain steamed rice.

What do you do with a leftover lamb roast? Try this lightly spiced Indian dish.

Jhal Farezi
Serves 4

- *1 tablespoon ghee or butter*
- *2 tablespoons oil*
- *2 onions, sliced*
- *1 teaspoon finely chopped garlic*
- *1 teaspoon finely grated fresh ginger*
- *1 teaspoon chilli powder or to taste*
- *1 teaspoon turmeric*
- *½ teaspoon ground black pepper*
- *1 teaspoon Garam Masala (see p. 78)*
- *salt to taste*
- *2 cups sliced cold meat*
- *4–6 quartered or sliced cooked potatoes*
- *squeeze of lemon juice*
- *chopped fresh mint or coriander*
- *sliced tomato and cucumber*

Heat ghee and oil in a frying pan or wok and fry onions on medium heat, stirring constantly, until they are deep brown. Add garlic and ginger and fry 1 minute longer, then add ground spices and salt and fry for a few seconds more. Add meat and potatoes and toss. Sprinkle with a few tablespoons of water, cover and heat through for 5 minutes.

Uncover and ensure that all liquid is evaporated. Sprinkle with lemon juice and herbs. Garnish with slices of tomato and cucumber and serve with steamed rice and a sweet chutney.

Long steaming ensures the pork is so tender it can be broken with chopsticks. Serve with plenty of steamed rice, because this dish is very rich.

STEAMED, LAYERED PORK
Serves 6 to 8

- *750 g (1½ lb) pork belly with layers of lean and fat*
- *1 teaspoon chopped garlic*
- *1 teaspoon sugar*
- *2 teaspoons chilli bean sauce*
- *1/3 cup dark soy sauce*
- *2 tablespoons dry sherry*
- *½ teaspoon five spice powder*
- *3 tablespoons roasted rice powder*

Have butcher remove skin and thick layer of fat next to it. Cut pork into large squares. Crush garlic with sugar to a smooth purée and mix with chilli bean sauce, soy sauce, sherry and five spice powder.

Pour mixture over pork, mix well and marinate for 2 hours. Roll pork in roasted rice powder and place in a heatproof dish. Steam over boiling water on high heat for 2 hours, replacing water with more boiling water as it boils away. When done, fat should be transparent and pork very tender. Serve hot with rice and stir-fried or steamed vegetables.

Very popular in Thailand, this Muslim dish originated in India.

MASAMAN CURRY
Serves 6 to 8

- *1.5 kg (3 lb) blade or other stewing steak*
- *6 cardamom pods*
- *2½ cups canned coconut milk*
- *4 tablespoons Masaman Curry Paste (see p. 83)*
- *8 small new potatoes, scrubbed*
- *10 small pickling onions, peeled*
- *3 tablespoons fish sauce*
- *3 tablespoons lime or lemon juice*
- *1 tablespoon palm sugar*
- *½ cup fresh basil leaves*
- *½ cup whole roasted peanuts*

Cut beef into large cubes and put into a pan with cardamom pods and 1½ cups of coconut milk diluted with an equal amount of water. Simmer until meat is almost tender.

Heat rest of undiluted coconut milk in a wok and reduce over medium heat, stirring, until thick and oily. Add Masaman Curry Paste and fry until fragrant. Add meat, potatoes, onions, fish sauce, lime or lemon juice and palm sugar. Cook until potatoes are done, adding some of stock from meat as required. Towards the end of cooking stir in basil leaves and peanuts. Serve with steamed rice.

Vegetables

In countries where much of the population is vegetarian, bland, overboiled vegetables do not exist. Judiciously spiced, some are made quite dry to use with flat bread or as a filling in lentil pancakes, others with a mild, soupy sauce to moisten a large helping of rice. Vegetables cooked the Asian way are particularly healthy because none of the goodness is thrown out with the cooking water.

Mashed potatoes with a difference—Indian style.

Spicy Mashed Potatoes
Serves 4 to 6

- 750 g (1½ lb) potatoes
- 1 tablespoon ghee or oil
- 1 teaspoon black mustard seeds
- 1 onion, finely chopped
- 1 or 2 fresh chillies, sliced
- ½ teaspoon ground turmeric
- 1 teaspoon Garam Masala (see p. 78)
- 1 teaspoon salt or to taste
- ¼ teaspoon chilli powder
- 2 tablespoons lemon juice
- ¼ cup chopped fresh mint or coriander

Boil potatoes in skins, peel while still hot and mash smoothly. Heat ghee and fry mustard seeds until they pop. Add onion and fresh chillies and fry until onion is soft and golden. Stir in turmeric, Garam Masala, salt and chilli powder and stir well for a few seconds, then add lemon juice and potatoes, mixing flavours in thoroughly and heating through. Serve sprinkled with fresh mint or coriander.

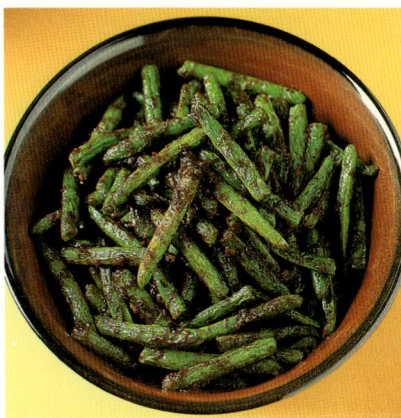

This flavoursome Burmese dish was one I came upon at the Mandalay restaurant in San Francisco. Here's a new slant on how good a bean can taste.

Deep Fried Green Beans
Serves 4 to 6

- 500 g (1 lb) tender green beans
- ½ cup peanut oil
- 2 tablespoons sesame oil
- 2 teaspoons crushed garlic
- 2 tablespoons dried shrimp powder, optional
- 1 teaspoon chilli powder
- 2 teaspoons dried tamarind pulp dissolved in ½ cup hot water
- 1 teaspoon fish sauce 2 teaspoons sugar

Top and tail beans, wash and dry well in a tea towel and cut into bite-size pieces. Heat peanut oil for deep–frying and when very hot, fry half the beans at a time, for just 2 minutes or until they blister. Remove with a slotted spoon and drain on paper towels.

Pour off all but a tablespoon of peanut oil. Add sesame oil and fry garlic over gentle heat until golden. Add shrimp and chilli powders and fry, stirring, for 3 or 4 minutes. Add tamarind, fish sauce and sugar, stir and simmer until reduced and oil shimmers on surface. Return beans to wok and toss until coated. Serve with hot steamed rice and other dishes.

Sayur, an Indonesian mildly spiced vegetable dish, is served with rice and a dry curry to round out a meal.

BEAN SAYUR
Serves 6

- *2 tablespoons peanut oil*
- *1 large onion, chopped*
- *3 cloves garlic, finely chopped*
- *3 fresh red chillies, seeded and chopped*
- *1 teaspoon dried shrimp paste*
- *1 stalk lemon grass, bruised*
- *2 teaspoons ground coriander*
- *1 teaspoon ground cummin*
- *1 teaspoon finely chopped galangal*
- *1 salam leaf or sprig of fresh curry leaves*
- *3 cups chicken stock or water*
- *1 cup canned coconut milk*
- *500 g (1 lb) snake beans or green beans, sliced*
- *salt to taste*

Heat oil in a large saucepan and fry onion, garlic, chillies and shrimp paste. Add lemon grass, coriander, cummin and galangal and fry, stirring, for 1 minute. Add salam leaf, stock and coconut milk and bring to the boil, stirring. Add beans and salt to taste. Bring to the boil and simmer until beans are tender. Shredded cabbage, sliced zucchini or a mixture of vegetables can be used in the same way.

Potato Curry with Tamarind
Serves 4 to 6

- *750 g (1½ lb) potatoes*
- *walnut-sized piece of dried tamarind pulp*
- *3 teaspoons brown sugar*
- *2 tablespoons ghee or oil*
- *1 teaspoon black mustard seeds*
- *1 teaspoon ground turmeric*
- *1 teaspoon chilli powder or to taste*
- *2 teaspoons ground coriander*
- *1 teaspoon ground cummin*
- *1 teaspoon salt or to taste*
- *2 or 3 fresh chillies, sliced*
- *2 tablespoons fresh grated or desiccated coconut*

Peel potatoes and cut into cubes. Soak tamarind in ½ cup hot water and when cool enough, squeeze firmly to dissolve pulp, strain through a nylon or stainless steel strainer and discard seeds and fibres. Dissolve sugar in tamarind liquid.

Heat ghee or oil and fry mustard seeds, add turmeric, chilli powder, coriander and cummin and stir over low heat for 1 minute. Add potatoes and toss to coat with spices. Add salt and ¼ cup water, cover with well-fitting lid and cook on very low heat for 15 minutes.

Stir in tamarind, chillies and coconut. Cover and cook until potatoes are tender. Serve with chapatis or rice.

Thai Eggplant Curry
Serves 4

- *500 g (1 lb) eggplant*
- *½ cup oil for deep-frying*
- *2 tablespoons Pepper and Coriander Paste (see p. 82)
  or Thai Green Curry Paste (see p. 81)*
- *1 cup canned coconut milk*
- *4 kaffir lime leaves*
- *1–2 tablespoons fish sauce*
- *1 tablespoon palm sugar*

Wash and dry eggplants but do not peel. If using slender eggplants, cut into slices, otherwise cut into large cubes. Deep-fry in hot oil until browned, remove and drain on paper towels.

In 1 tablespoon oil fry Pepper and Coriander Paste or Thai Green Curry Paste over low heat, stirring, until fragrant. Add coconut milk and 1 cup water, lime leaves, fish sauce and palm sugar. Stir and simmer for 5 minutes, then add eggplant and simmer for 10 minutes longer or until eggplant is tender. Serve with rice.

Quite a famous dish, this is a perfect example of how to put zip into an ingredient as bland as bean curd.

MA PO DOU FU
Serves 4

- *3 pieces dried wood fungus*
- *500 g (1 lb) firm bean curd*
- *3 tablespoons peanut oil*
- *2 tablespoons finely chopped fresh ginger*
- *2 teaspoons finely chopped garlic*
- *1/3 cup chopped spring onion*
- *125 g (4 oz) minced pork*
- *1 cup chicken or pork stock*
- *1 teaspoon chilli bean sauce, or to taste*
- *1 tablespoon ground bean sauce*
- *2 tablespoons tomato ketchup*
- *2 teaspoons cornflour*
- *2 teaspoons oriental sesame oil*

Soak wood fungus in cold water for 10 minutes until swollen, cut into bite-size pieces, discarding any woody portions. Dice bean curd, drop into boiling water and let water return to boil for a few minutes to heat bean curd through, then drain in a colander.

Heat oil in a wok and fry ginger, garlic and spring onion over medium heat, stirring, until fragrant. Add pork and stir-fry, pressing it against side of wok until it is no longer pink. Mix stock, chilli bean sauce, ground bean sauce and tomato ketchup, pour into wok and simmer for 5 minutes. Mix cornflour with a tablespoon of cold water and stir into sauce until it boils and thickens.

Gently stir in drained bean curd, wood fungus and sesame oil, heat through and serve on steamed rice. Garnish with red chilli if liked.

Any favourite vegetable can be cooked in this light coconut sauce— pumpkin, cauliflower, zucchini, asparagus, okra. It is also suitable as a sauce for hard-boiled eggs or omelette.

WHITE VEGETABLE CURRY
Serves 6

- *2 cups canned coconut milk*
- *2 medium onions, sliced*
- *3 fresh green chillies*
- *1 teaspoon ground turmeric*
- *3 cloves garlic, chopped*
- *6 slices fresh ginger*
- *1 small cinnamon stick*
- *4 strips pandan leaf*
- *1 stem lemon grass, finely sliced or 3 strips lemon rind*
- *2 sprigs fresh curry leaves*
- *750 g (1½ lb) sliced vegetables*

Put 1 cup coconut milk and 1½ cups water into a saucepan with all ingredients except vegetables. Simmer gently, uncovered, about 10 minutes. Add vegetables and salt to taste and cook until vegetables are tender. Add remaining cup of coconut milk, stir in gently, heat through and serve with rice and other curries.

Rice, Bread, Noodles and Accompaniments

The poorer countries of the world often have highly spiced and seasoned food. There are several reasons for this. Where temperatures are high and refrigeration unavailable, spices are used to preserve food. Unlike first world countries, where protein-rich meat, fish, poultry and dairy products are plentiful, the staple diet is grain and that grain is most often rice. There is no denying that, indispensable as it is, rice is a bland food—thus hot, spicy, sour and salty flavours create the perfect lift.

It is a popular Western misconception, however, that rice, bread or noodles are only accompaniments to meat, poultry or fish. In fact in Asia, they are staples—spicy side-dishes are the accompaniments—and the amount consumed is considered all important. There should be 3 or 4 times as much rice, bread or noodles eaten as curry, stir-fry or braise. The starch in these staples helps assuage the effect of the strong spices and rich gravies on the digestive system.

This section also includes a creamy raita to soothe the palate; hot, piquant sambals; and flavoursome chutneys and pickles.

In India this unleavened wholemeal bread is cooked on a griddle called a tawa. *A heavy-based frying pan or griddle plate can be used instead.*

CHAPATIS
Makes 18 to 20

- *3 cups atta or roti flour*
- *salt to taste*
- *1 tablespoon ghee*
- *1 cup lukewarm water*

Put flour into a mixing bowl. Mix in salt, then rub in ghee. Add water all at once and mix to a firm but not stiff dough. Knead dough for about 10 minutes—longer kneading will give lighter bread. (You can also make dough in a food processor to reduce kneading time.) Shape dough into a ball, cover with clear plastic wrap and let stand for at least 1 hour.

Form dough into walnut-size balls. Roll out each one on a lightly floured board to a very thin circle. Once all are rolled, heat a griddle plate or frying pan and cook chapatis, starting with those that were rolled first (resting time makes the chapatis lighter). Place chapati on griddle and leave for about 1 minute. Turn and cook other side for a further minute, pressing lightly around edges with a folded tea towel. This encourages bubbles to form. As each one is cooked, wrap immediately in a clean, dry tea towel until all are ready.

Have the oil moderately hot for this Indian deep-fried wholemeal bread
so it fries without absorbing too much oil and becoming greasy.

PURIS
Makes 24

Proceed as for Chapatis (see p. 60) but make discs smaller, about the size of a small saucer. When all of dough is rolled into rounds, pour a depth of about 2.5 cm (1 inch) oil into a deep frying pan. Heat oil until a faint haze rises from surface. Fry puris one at a time over moderate heat, spooning hot oil continually over surface of each, as this makes them puff and swell. Turn over and fry other side. When pale golden brown on both sides, remove and drain on paper towels. Serve immediately with curries.

Note   When rolling out chapatis, puris and parathas, please remember to keep them separate. If allowed to touch they will stick together. If space dictates they have to be stacked, sprinkle each with flour and lay a square of greaseproof paper over. Make sure paper is large enough to cover the whole circle of dough, otherwise the unprotected ends will attach themselves to the next circle and spoil the nice round shape.

Rich, flaky and deliciously flavoured with ghee, the paratha is a popular Indian bread.

PARATHA
Makes 16

- 2 cups fine wholemeal flour
- 2 cups plain flour
- 1½ teaspoons salt
- 8 tablespoons ghee
- extra ghee for cooking

Sieve flours and salt into a mixing bowl and rub in 2 tablespoons of ghee. Add 1½ cups lukewarm water, mix and knead dough for at least 10 minutes (the more it is kneaded, the lighter the bread will be). Form dough into a ball, cover with clear plastic wrap and set aside for 1 hour.

Divide dough into 16 equal portions and roll each into a smooth ball. Melt remaining ghee and allow to cool slightly. Roll out each ball of dough on a lightly floured board into a very thin circle. Put 2 teaspoons of ghee in centre of each and spread lightly by hand. With a knife make a cut from centre of circle to outer edge. Starting at cut edge, roll dough closely into a cone shape. Pick up, press apex and base of cone towards each other and flatten slightly. You will now have a small roughly circular lump of dough again. Lightly flour board and roll out dough very gently, not as thinly as the first time. Take care not to press too hard or air will come out at edges. Parathas should be as round as possible.

Cook on a hot griddle or in a heavy pan liberally greased with extra ghee, turning parathas and spreading with more ghee, until golden brown. Serve hot.

Rice cooked by the absorption method is used in Chinese and Japanese meals, and it should be short or medium grain rice. The result is easy to eat with chopsticks as the grains cling together. It is important to cook the rice in a heavy-based saucepan.

STEAMED SHORT GRAIN RICE
Serves 6

- *2½ cups short or medium grain rice*
- *3 cups cold water*

Wash rice several times in cold water. Leave to drain in a sieve or colander for at least 30 minutes. Place rice in a heavy-based saucepan with a well-fitting lid. Add cold water and bring rapidly to the boil. Cover pan, turn heat very low and cook for 15 minutes without lifting lid. Turn heat high for 20 seconds, and, still without uncovering, remove pan from heat and set aside to stand for 10 minutes before serving.

Those with a preference for long grain rice with its separate grains and fluffier consistency have a lot of choice. The current favourite is jasmine rice—not a brand name but a variety grown in Thailand. In India, especially in the southern, central and eastern areas where rice forms the major part of a meal, there are numerous varieties. Long grain rice (in particular aromatic basmati or Dehra Dun) is used for pilau or biriani and is popular as plain rice served with curries.

STEAMED LONG GRAIN RICE
Serves 4 to 6

- 2½ cups basmati or other long grain rice
- 2 teaspoons ghee, optional
- 2 teaspoons salt or to taste, optional

Wash rice well and soak for 1 hour in cold water (generally rice grown and processed in Australia or America does not need washing). Drain rice in a sieve for 30 minutes at least.

Bring 3½ cups water to the boil in a heavy saucepan with ghee and salt. Add rice, stir, and bring back quickly to the boil. Reduce heat to very low, cover pan tightly (use a sheet of foil, if necessary, to make lid fit tightly) and cook for 15 to 20 minutes. Do not lift lid during this time. Remove lid and allow steam to escape for 5 minutes. Carefully fluff rice with a fork—be careful not to mash grains, which should be firm and separate, yet tender. Serve with a slotted metal spoon to avoid crushing grains.

This spicy pilau can be served alone, accompanied by pickles, pappadams and a raita or served as part of a curry meal.

RICE COOKED IN MEAT STOCK
Serves 4 to 6

- 2½ cups basmati rice
- 3 lamb shanks
- 6 cardamom pods, bruised
- ½ teaspoon whole black peppercorns
- 1 large, dried red chilli
- 2 medium onions
- 4 whole cloves
- 2 teaspoons salt or to taste
- ⅓ cup ghee
- ¼ teaspoon saffron strands, toasted and crushed
- 2 green chillies, finely chopped
- 2 cloves garlic, finely chopped
- 1 teaspoon finely grated fresh ginger
- 1 teaspoon Garam Masala (see p. 78)
- 3 tablespoons rose water or ¼ teaspoon rose essence
- ½ cup sultanas
- ¼ cup toasted cashew nuts
- 3 hard-boiled eggs, quartered
- mint leaves

Wash rice well in several changes of water, drain and set aside in colander to dry for at least 1 hour.

Place lamb in a saucepan with cardamom pods, peppercorns and dried chilli. Peel onions and stud one with cloves. Add this to pan with plenty of water to cover. Season with salt and bring to the boil. Lower heat and simmer gently for 2 hours. Cool slightly, strain stock and measure 4 cups. Remove meat from bones. Cut into bite-size pieces and set aside.

Slice remaining onion and fry in ghee in a large saucepan until golden. Add chillies, garlic and ginger and fry, stirring constantly, for 1 minute. Stir in rice and fry 3 minutes more, turning carefully with a slotted metal spoon so as not to break up the rice grains. Add hot stock, saffron and lamb pieces, Garam Masala, rose water, sultanas and salt to taste. Stir until well mixed. Cover pan tightly and simmer over very low heat for 20 minutes. At end of cooking time remove pan from heat and let stand uncovered for 5 minutes. Gently fluff rice with a fork and transfer to serving dish. Serve garnished with cashews, hard-boiled eggs and mint leaves.

For Indian feasts, rice is layered with chicken or lamb curry–a one-dish meal known as Biriani. Good for making ahead and reheating, and convenient for entertaining.

BIRIANI
Serves 12 to 14

- *Double quantity Rice Cooked in Meat Stock (see p. 65)*
- *1 quantity Lamb Curry (see p. 40)*
or One-Hundred Almond Curry (see p. 25)

Prepare rice and chosen curry. Grease a large ovenproof dish with ghee and make 3 layers of rice and 2 of curry, finishing with rice. Press foil to surface of rice and cover with lid. Heat through in moderately low oven for 1 hour. Uncover and garnish with nuts, eggs and mint. Serve with raita and chutney.

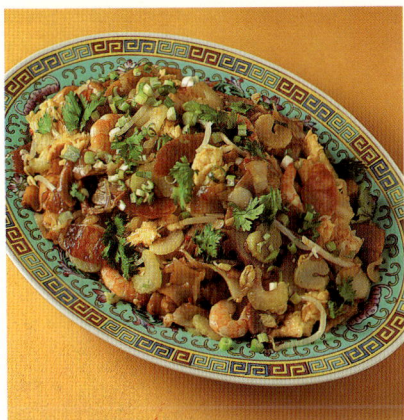

Fried Rice Noodles
Serves 6

- 1 kg (2 lb) *fresh rice noodles or 500 g (1 lb) dried rice noodles*
- 2 Chinese sausages (lap cheong)
- 125 g (4 oz) barbecued pork
- 250 g (8 oz) small raw prawns
- 1 cup fresh bean sprouts
- ¼ cup peanut oil
- 3 cloves garlic, chopped finely
- 2 medium onions, sliced
- 4 fresh red chillies, seeded and chopped
- 2 teaspoons fresh ginger, finely chopped
- 1 stalk celery, finely sliced
- 2 tablespoons oyster sauce
- 2 tablespoons dark soy sauce
- 3 eggs, beaten
- 4 spring onions, chopped
- 2 tablespoons fresh coriander leaves

Slice fresh noodles into strips approximately the width of a pencil. If using dried noodles, boil and drain. Steam sausages for about 10 minutes or until plump and translucent. Cut into very thin diagonal slices. Thinly slice barbecued pork. Shell and devein prawns. Pinch any straggly tails from bean sprouts.

Heat half the oil in a wok and stir-fry garlic, onions, chillies and ginger over medium heat until soft. Add sausages, pork and prawns and fry for about 2 minutes or until prawns become opaque. Add bean sprouts and celery, toss quickly, then remove mixture from wok and set aside. Pour in beaten eggs and stir constantly until set. Remove from wok.

Heat remaining oil in wok and when very hot, add noodles and stir fry until heated through. Add oyster and soy sauces and toss until well mixed. Return fried mixture to wok and toss until all ingredients are well mixed. Serve hot garnished with spring onions and coriander leaves.

CHILLI CHICKEN NOODLES
Serves 3 to 4

- *250 g (8 oz) egg noodles*
- *250 g (8 oz) chicken fillets*
- *2 tablespoons peanut oil*
- *2 teaspoons finely chopped garlic*
- *1 teaspoon chilli bean sauce*
- *1 tablespoon sweet chilli sauce*
- *1 tablespoon light soy sauce*
- *2 tablespoons lime juice*
- *¼ cup chopped spring onions or coriander leaves*

Cook noodles in lightly salted boiling water until tender, drain in colander and run cold water through to stop cooking. Slice or dice chicken finely. Heat peanut oil and fry garlic over low heat until fragrant and pale golden. Add chilli bean sauce and chicken and stir-fry until chicken is no longer pink. Add sweet chilli sauce, soy sauce and lime juice, toss until chicken is cooked. Add noodles and spring onions to wok and toss until thoroughly mixed. Serve at once.

Note If dried egg noodles are purchased in little bundles, soak them in warm water for 10 minutes to loosen the strands, otherwise the inner strands stick together and do not cook evenly.

Pappadams

These spicy lentil wafers can be served as a snack or appetiser, or used as an accompaniment to rice and curry dishes. They are best cooked shortly before serving, but can also be prepared a few hours before, left to cool and then stored in an airtight container. These days I prefer to cook pappadams in the microwave—no oil is used, and if 4 are cooked at a time on full power, they are done in 2 minutes. Turn each a half circle after 1 minute. The best pappadams to use for microwaving are the north Indian type, usually with a smooth, slightly shiny surface, as opposed to a floury surface.

If no microwave is available, fry them the old-fashioned way. Heat oil for deep-frying until hot and then deep-fry one pappadam at a time for a few seconds. They will swell immediately and become pale gold in colour. Drain well on paper towels.

Extra large lentil wafers are used in this recipe and, like the smaller variety, can be found in packets in Asian food stores. Some have spicy flavourings such as peppercorns and chilli in the lentil mixture.

Garnished Pappadams

- *6 large pappadams*
- *½ cup freshly grated coconut*
- *2 tablespoons finely chopped coriander leaves*
- *chilli powder to taste*

Cook pappadams by preferred method and just before serving sprinkle each with coconut, coriander and chilli powder and serve immediately as an accompaniment to curries and rice.

If garnished too far ahead, they lose their delightful crispness.

Store this pickle in the refrigerator. For those who like it hot, serve as it is. Or extend it by mixing 1 part pickle with 2 parts plain yoghurt and serving it as a milder flavoured relish with a meal of rice and curry.

FRIED EGGPLANT PICKLE
Makes 2 cups

- *1 kg (2 lb) eggplants*
- *1–2 teaspoons salt*
- *1 teaspoon turmeric*
- *1½ cups oil*
- *12 large, dried red chillies*
- *4 cloves garlic*
- *1 tablespoon chopped fresh ginger*
- *2 tablespoons black mustard seeds*
- *2 teaspoons ground coriander*
- *½ cup brown sugar*
- *¾ cup vinegar*
- *2 teaspoons Fragrant Garam Masala (see p. 78)*

Wash eggplants and cut into cubes. Sprinkle with salt and turmeric and leave in a colander for 30 minutes to draw out excess liquid. Blot dry on kitchen paper and deep-fry in 1¼ cups oil until brown. Remove to a bowl.

Soak chillies in hot water for 5 minutes (reserve liquid). Place chillies, garlic, ginger, mustard seeds, coriander and a little of the chilli water into a blender and process until puréed.

Heat ¼ cup oil and fry blended mixture for a few minutes. Stir in eggplant, cover and cook over low heat, stirring occasionally, until eggplant is soft. Add sugar and vinegar and simmer until mixture is thick, stirring occasionally to prevent burning. Stir in Fragrant Garam Masala. Leave to cool, then put into sterilised jar.

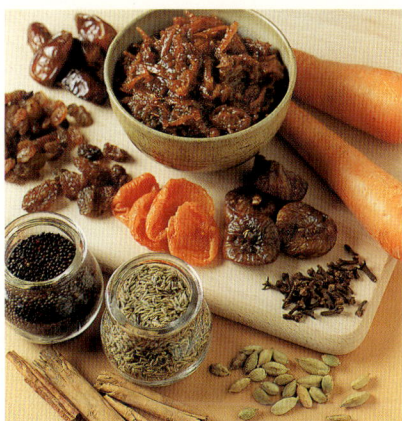

A sweet and spicy pickle served at Parsi weddings.

PARSI WEDDING PICKLE
Makes about 3 cups

- ½ cup stoned, chopped dates
- ½ cup raisins
- ½ cup chopped dried apricots
- ½ cup chopped dried figs
- 500 g (1 lb) carrots
- 2 teaspoons cummin seeds
- 2 small cinnamon sticks
- 20 cardamom pods, bruised
- ¼ teaspoon ground cloves
- 2 cups vinegar
- 2 cups brown sugar
- 3 teaspoons salt
- 2 teaspoons chilli powder
- 2 teaspoons ground black mustard seeds
- 2 cloves garlic, crushed
- 1 teaspoon grated fresh ginger

Soak dried fruits in 1 cup water for 1 hour. Wash and peel carrots and grate finely. Put all ingredients into a non-aluminium saucepan and bring slowly to the boil, stirring frequently. Simmer until fruit is very soft and liquid syrupy. Remove whole spices. Cool and store in sterilised jars.

A raita is the ideal accompaniment for hot curries—its cool yoghurt base provides a perfect foil for pungent spices.

CUCUMBER RAITA
Serves 6

- 1 large, seedless green cucumber (see Note)
- salt to taste
- 1 small clove garlic, crushed
- ¼ cup sliced mint leaves
- 1 cup plain yoghurt
- ½ cup thick sour cream
- lime juice to taste
- ½ teaspoon roasted cummin seeds

Wash cucumber, score skin and slice very thinly. Place in a bowl, sprinkle with salt and chill for 1 hour. Pour off liquid, pressing cucumbers to extract as much as possible. Mix garlic and mint leaves with yoghurt and sour cream, then stir into cucumbers and mix thoroughly. Add more salt if necessary, and lime juice. Sprinkle with cummin seeds and chill until ready to serve. Garnish with a mint sprig if desired.

Note   You can substitute 2 large, peeled and shredded green apples for the cucumber. Don't sprinkle them with salt, but toss them in with lime juice as soon as they are shredded to prevent browning.

CHILLI OIL PICKLE
Makes about 4 cups

- *1 kg (2 lb) long green chillies*
- *2 tablespoons salt*
- *1 tablespoon ground turmeric*
- *1½ tablespoons black mustard seeds*
- *¼ cup vinegar*
- *2 tablespoons chopped garlic*
- *2 cups mustard seed oil*
- *1 teaspoon fenugreek seeds*
- *2 teaspoons nigella seeds (kalonji)*
- *2 teaspoons crushed asafoetida*
- *1 small cinnamon stick*

Wash and dry chillies. Cut off and discard stalks and slice chillies across into 1 cm (½ inch) slices. Place in a bowl, sprinkle with salt and turmeric and toss until well mixed. Cover and leave for 2 days and if possible place in the sun for a few hours each day. Soak mustard seeds in vinegar overnight, then purée with garlic in a blender.

Heat oil in a large pan and fry fenugreek and nigella seeds, stirring, until fenugreek is golden brown. Add asafoetida, stir once, then add blended mixture, cinnamon stick and chillies with liquid they exude. Cook, stirring occasionally, until oil rises to surface and chillies are cooked. Do not let them become too soft. Cool and transfer to a sterilised jar.

This is not a bird, but a pungent dried fish which is served as an accompaniment to curries and rice.

BOMBAY DUCK CHILLI FRY
Serves 4

- *6 pieces Bombay duck (see Note)*
- *4 tablespoons peanut oil*
- *2 onions, finely sliced*
- *3 or 4 large dried chillies*
- *lemon juice to taste*
- *½ teaspoon sugar or to taste*

Cut dried fish into pieces and deep-fry in oil. Drain on absorbent paper. Fry onions until golden. Wearing rubber gloves, break off stems of chillies, shake out seeds. Snip into short lengths and add to onions, stir and fry for 3 or 4 minutes longer. Add lemon juice and sugar to taste and serve at room temperature as a hot sambal to be eaten in very small quantities.

Note   This fish is cut into pieces about 5 cm (2 inches) long and deep-fried in hot oil until light golden brown. Sold in packets.

ONION SAMBAL

- *2 medium red or purple onions*
- *1 teaspoon chilli powder*
- *1 teaspoon roasted cummin seeds*
- *salt to taste*
- *lime or lemon juice to taste*

Cut onions into fine slices. Place in a bowl and sprinkle with chilli powder, cummin seeds, salt and lime juice. Toss lightly until well mixed. Make just before serving to accompany curries and rice.

This sauce base is diluted with coconut milk or water to give a pouring consistency, but in its undiluted form makes a wonderful spread for savoury crackers or tiny, bite-size sandwiches as a cocktail savoury.

Peanut Sauce
Makes about 2½ cups

- ½ cup peanut oil
- 1 tablespoon dried garlic flakes
- 3 tablespoons crisp fried onions
- 3 or 4 large, dried red chillies
- 1 teaspoon dried shrimp paste
- 2 tablespoons dark soy sauce
- 2 tablespoons strained lime juice
- 1 x 375 g (12 oz) jar crunchy peanut butter
- 2 tablespoons coarse sugar (raw sugar or coffee crystals)

Heat oil and fry garlic flakes on gentle heat until pale gold, remove immediately with a slotted spoon or lower into oil on a fine mesh strainer so you can lift them out as soon as they turn pale gold. Drain on absorbent paper.

Fry chillies quite slowly until puffed, crisp and quite dark in colour. Drain and cool, then discard stems and crumble or chop chillies into small pieces. If using ready-fried onions, simply crush into bits.

In same oil cook shrimp paste, crushing with back of

spoon. Add soy sauce and lime juice and stir to dissolve. Remove from heat. Stir in peanut butter and allow to cool completely before mixing in fried garlic, onions, chillies and sugar. Store in a wide-mouthed jar in refrigerator. Heat ½ cup of sauce base and add about ½ cup diluted coconut milk or water to give a pouring consistency.

Sweet and hot at the same time, this popular sauce can be tamed by adding an equal quantity of tomato ketchup.

GARLIC CHILLI SAUCE
Makes about 4 cups

- 250 g (8 oz) fresh red chillies
- 750 g (1½ lb) white sugar
- 1 x 750 mL (26 fl oz) bottle white vinegar
- 375 g (12 oz) sultanas
- 10–15 cloves garlic, peeled
- 2 tablespoons finely grated fresh ginger
- 3 teaspoons salt or to taste

Wear rubber gloves when handling chillies. Cut off and discard stems and, if preferred, cut chillies down centre and scrape out seeds.

In a non-aluminium saucepan combine all ingredients and simmer until chillies, garlic and sultanas are very soft. Cool and purée in food processor or push through a sieve. Pour into sterilised bottles and seal.

Spice Mixtures and Curry Pastes

Here is the key to producing Asian meals in very little time. Every couple of months go shopping for fresh ingredients, make and store the pastes. If you love Asian food and eat it often, keep pastes in refrigerator but if you cook it not so frequently, divide pastes into meal-size portions, usually about ¼ cup, wrap and freeze. Don't forget to label them carefully.

'Panch' is the Hindi word for 'five' and this aromatic mixture consists of five different seeds that are used whole.

Whole Spice Mix (Panch Phora)
Makes about ½ cup

- *2 tablespoons black mustard seeds*
- *2 tablespoons cummin seeds*
- *2 tablespoons kalonji (nigella) seeds*
- *1 tablespoon fenugreek seeds*
- *1 tablespoon fennel seeds*

Mix all ingredients and put into a jar with airtight lid. Shake before use to ensure seeds are evenly distributed.

GARAM MASALA
Makes about ¾ cup

- *4 tablespoons coriander seeds*
- *2 tablespoons cummin seeds*
- *1 tablespoon whole black peppercorns*
- *2 teaspoons cardamom seeds (measure after roasting and removing from pods)*
- *4 x 7.5 cm (3 inch) cinnamon sticks*
- *1 teaspoon whole cloves*
- *1 whole nutmeg*

Roast each whole spice separately, except for nutmeg, in a small, heavy-based pan. Turn each one out onto a plate to cool as soon as it smells fragrant. Peel and discard pods from roasted cardamoms, using only seeds. Grind all ingredients in a blender to a fine powder. Finely grate nutmeg and mix in. Store in glass jar with airtight lid.

FRAGRANT GARAM MASALA
Makes about ¼ cup

- *3 x 7.5 cm (3 inch) cinnamon sticks*
- *2 teaspoons cardamom seeds (measure after removing pods)*
- *1 teaspoon whole cloves*
- *1 teaspoon blades of mace*

Roast spices separately in a small, heavy-based pan as in the recipe for Garam Masala (see above). When cool, grind in a blender or with a mortar and pestle. Store in an airtight jar.

Asian spice stores sell Ceylon curry powder—it differs from other spice mixtures in that the spices are first roasted until dark brown. You can make your own curry powder, however, with the following recipe.

CEYLON CURRY POWDER
Makes about 1½ cups

- *1 cup coriander seeds*
- *½ cup cummin seeds*
- *1 tablespoon fennel seeds*
- *1 teaspoon fenugreek seeds*
- *1 x 5 cm (2 inches) cinnamon stick*
- *1 teaspoon whole cloves*
- *1 teaspoon cardamom seeds*
- *2 tablespoons dried curry leaves*
- *2 teaspoons chilli powder, optional*
- *2 tablespoons ground rice, optional*

Roast separately coriander, cummin, fennel and fenugreek in a dry pan over low heat, stirring constantly, until each one turns a fairly dark brown. Do not let them burn. Put into a blender container with cinnamon stick broken into pieces, cloves, cardamom and curry leaves. Blend on high speed until finely powdered. Mix with chilli powder and ground rice if used. Store in an airtight jar.

Buy good quality whole spices and, once ground, store the mixtures in airtight jars in a cool, dry and dark cupboard. This will help to preserve the flavour and fragrance.

THAI RED CURRY PASTE
Makes about 1 cup

- 4–6 dried red chillies
- 2 small brown onions, chopped
- 1 teaspoon black peppercorns
- 2 teaspoons ground cummin
- 1 tablespoon ground coriander
- 2 tablespoons chopped fresh coriander, including root
- 1 teaspoon salt
- 1 stem lemon grass, finely sliced or 2 teaspoons chopped lemon rind
- 2 teaspoons chopped galangal in brine
- 1 tablespoon chopped garlic
- 2 teaspoons dried shrimp paste
- 1 teaspoon turmeric
- 2 teaspoons paprika (see Note)

Remove stems from chillies (if you want curry to be as hot as it is in Thailand, leave seeds in). Break chillies into pieces, soak in just enough water to cover for 10 minutes, then place in an electric blender with remaining ingredients. Purée, stopping frequently to push ingredients down with a spatula. You might need to add extra water to assist with blending.

Note Even though paprika is not used in Thailand, I have added it to give the curry the requisite red colour without using the traditional number of red chillies. If you're a seasoned chilli eater and are sure of the spice tolerance of the people you are cooking for, adjust the recipe accordingly.

Thai Green Curry Paste
Makes about 1 cup

- 4 large or 8 small green chillies
- 1 medium onion, chopped
- 1 tablespoon chopped garlic
- ½ cup chopped fresh coriander, including roots, stems and leaves
- ¼ cup finely sliced lemon grass, or thinly peeled rind of 1 lemon
- 1 tablespoon chopped galangal, fresh or bottled
- 2 teaspoons ground coriander
- 1 teaspoon ground cummin
- 1 teaspoon black peppercorns
- 1 teaspoon ground turmeric
- 1 teaspoon dried shrimp paste

With rubber gloves, remove stems and roughly chop chillies. Put into an electric blender with remaining ingredients and purée. Add a little water if necessary to help blending.

You can store this curry paste in an airtight jar in refrigerator for up to a month, or divide into convenient portions, wrap and freeze. Use as needed for other Thai curry dishes.

Pepper and Coriander Paste is one of the most useful items to have in the refrigerator. It keeps very well, but if you don't want to use it as fast as I do, it may be wise to add 1 teaspoon citric acid dissolved in a tablespoon or so of hot water.

PEPPER AND CORIANDER PASTE
Makes about 1 cup

- 1 tablespoon chopped garlic
- 2 teaspoons salt
- 2 tablespoons whole black peppercorns
- 2 cups coarsely chopped fresh coriander, including roots
- 2 tablespoons lemon juice

Crush garlic with salt to a smooth paste. Roast peppercorns in a dry pan for 1 or 2 minutes, then coarsely crush in a mortar and pestle. Finely chop coriander roots, leaves and stems. Mix all ingredients.

You can make this paste in a blender, but reduce black peppercorns to 1 tablespoon, as they are hotter when more finely ground. Store in an airtight jar in the refrigerator.

Note Some of the ways I use this paste include marinating chicken fillets with a good thick coating of it for 1 hour, then cooking them on the barbecue. Or, if I want a quick green chutney and don't have any fresh herbs on hand, stir a spoonful of the paste into a cup of natural yoghurt. If you run out of Thai Green Curry Paste never hesitate to use Pepper and Coriander Paste instead.

Masaman curry is spicy but sweet. Popular in Thailand, it has its origins in India. This paste is useful to save preparation time.

MASAMAN CURRY PASTE
Makes about 1 cup

- 10 large, dried red chillies
- 2 tablespoons oil
- 2 large onions, finely chopped
- 1 tablespoon chopped garlic
- 2 teaspoons dried shrimp paste
- 2 stems lemon grass, finely sliced
- 1 tablespoon chopped greater galangal
- 2 teaspoons chopped lesser galangal
- 2 tablespoons ground coriander
- 1 tablespoon ground cummin
- 2 teaspoons ground fennel
- 1 teaspoon ground cinnamon
- 1 teaspoon ground cardamom
- 1 teaspoon ground mace or nutmeg
- ½ teaspoon ground cloves

Wearing gloves, snip off stems of chillies and shake out the seeds (or leave them in if you like hot curries). Soak in boiling water for 10 minutes.

Heat oil and fry onions and garlic over gentle heat until golden. Add shrimp paste and fry a little longer. Allow to cool.

In an electric blender purée fried mixture with soaked chillies and a little of the soaking water, lemon grass and galangal.

Roast coriander, cummin and fennel in a dry pan, stirring frequently—do not let them burn. When fragrant turn out onto a plate and cool. Combine with cinnamon, cardamom, mace or nutmeg and cloves and stir into puréed ingredients. Bottle in an airtight jar and store in refrigerator for up to 4 weeks.

One of those useful pastes to have in the refrigerator which are so much nicer than the commercial versions since we add no preservatives or additives. Add a spoonful to vegetables, stir into rice with the liquid, or add to any Indian curry for an extra boost of fresh herb flavour.

GREEN MASALA PASTE
Makes about 2 cups

- 1 teaspoon fenugreek seeds
- 8 cloves garlic
- 2 tablespoons chopped fresh ginger
- 1 cup firmly packed fresh mint sprigs
- 1 small bunch fresh coriander
- ½ cup vinegar
- 3 teaspoons salt
- 2 teaspoons turmeric
- 1 teaspoon ground cardamom
- ½ teaspoon ground cloves
- ½ cup vegetable oil
- ½ cup sesame oil

Soak fenugreek seeds in ¼ cup water overnight. Combine in blender with all ingredients except oils. Blend on high speed until a smooth puree.

Heat vegetable oil and when very hot add puree and stir until mixture boils, then turn off heat. Cool, stir in sesame oil and pout into a glass jar. If oil does not cover the mixture add more sesame oil so surface has a layer of oil over it. Use a clean dry spoon to take paste from jar.

GLOSSARY

These ingredients are available in Asian food stores, but most of them are also sold in supermarkets.

ASAFOETIDA The dried, resinous gum of a plant that grows in Afghanistan and Iran. Widely used in Indian lentil dishes, for flavour and anti-flatulent effect. Sold in Indian stores. No substitute.

ATTA Fine wholemeal flour (or an 80:20 mixture of wholemeal and white) favoured for making chapatis and flat breads. Sold in Indian and some health food stores. Substitute fine wholemeal mixed with plain white flour.

BEAN SAUCE There are two kinds sold in glass jars: one is smooth, labelled 'refined bean sauce'; the other contains pieces of soy bean. Substitute dark soy sauce.

CARDAMOM Strongly fragrant seed pods of a plant of the ginger family, there are two kinds—large black pods or small green pods. Use the latter, bruised slightly to release fragrance. For ground cardamom, open pods and pound the small brown or black seeds inside with a mortar and pestle.

CHILLIES Wear gloves when chopping, slicing or removing seeds of fresh chillies, as the volatile oils can cause much discomfort. Small chillies are the hottest. It is possible to buy fresh, chopped chillies in jars or substitute sambal ulek (oelek). which is a mixture of fresh chillies and salt, or Tabasco Pepper Sauce (use 1 teaspoon for each hot chilli). Where large, dried chillies are called for, use the Asian variety, not the mild Californian or Mexican kind. Chilli powder also varies in intensity, depending on the chillies it is made from.

CHILLI BEAN SAUCE A super hot mixture of salted soy beans and chillies in oil. Use sparingly.

SWEET CHILLI SAUCE Looks like tomato ketchup except for the chilli seeds, which some brands retain in the sauce. There are many varieties, all varying in heat and sweetness. Some contain garlic and ginger.

CINNAMON Too often the thick, woody bark of cassia, which has a strong flavour and dark colour, is sold as cinnamon. True cinnamon is pale brown and much thinner, almost like parchment, and usually comprises 4 or 5 layers of this fine bark rolled into quills.

CLOVES The dried flower buds of a native South-East Asian tree, which contain a powerful antiseptic oil that keeps meats from putrefying—used for over 2000 years as a preservative as well as a flavouring. Use sparingly as they can overpower other flavours. Nearest substitute is allspice.

COCONUT MILK Readily available but some brands of canned coconut milk are thick and rich, others very thin. Mix the former with at least an equal amount of water, use the latter undiluted.

CORIANDER The finely ground, dried seeds are used in almost every curry. Sometimes they are roasted first to subtly emphasize the flavour. The fresh herb is also used and in Thailand the herb's root is an important flavour in curry pastes. Use the leaves as garnish and for extra flavour.

CUMMIN Sold as whole seeds or ground, this spice has a lemony fragrance and is a major component of curries.

CURRY LEAVES Small leaves making up a compound leaf, these have great flavour. Some nurseries and Asian stores now sell the plant. They will grow in a temperate climate if sheltered from frosts. Fresh leaves are preferable to dried.

FENNEL SEEDS Larger and lighter coloured than cummin, with a licorice flavour.

Fenugreek seeds   One of the essential ingredients in curry powder, these pale beige seeds have a bitter undertone. Use in small quantities.

Galangal   There are two species of galangal—greater and lesser. Greater galangal is similar in size and appearance to ginger. Galangal is sold in jars or frozen, dried or powdered, the latter being known as laos powder. Laos, lengkuas, kha are some of its local names. Some Asian food stores may even sell it fresh. Lesser galangal is sold bottled in brine, either whole or shredded into fine julienne strips. Also sold dried and ground it is most likely to be labelled its Indonesian name 'kencur' (kentjur).

Hoi sin sauce   A thick, dark, sweet bean sauce.

Kaffir lime leaves   Essential ingredient available fresh, frozen or dried.

Kalonji seeds (nigella)   Sold mostly in Indian food stores. Small black seeds with a little point on one end. It has a lovely nutty flavour and will keep indefinitely in an airtight jar. An essential part of Indian whole spice mix, panch phora. No substitute.

Palm sugar   Obtained from various tropical palms, it has a distinctive flavour but can be substituted by brown sugar.

Rice powder, roasted   This gives a distinctive flavour to certain dishes and should not be omitted. It is sold in small packets in some Asian shops, particularly those which carry Thai and Vietnamese ingredients. If unavailable you can make it by roasting rice grains over low heat in a heavy pan for about 15 minutes until a deep golden brown. Stir constantly so they don't burn. Cool, then grind to powder in blender.

Saffron   Try to get true saffron because there are imitations and nothing else has the same flavour. Expensive, but very little is needed. Keeps well if stored airtight. Best to buy the strands which are the dried stigmas of the autumn crocus, or tiny packets of powder. Distrust cheap saffron—there is no such thing.

Sesame oil   The sesame oil used in Eastern recipes is oriental sesame oil made from toasted sesame seeds. It is therefore dark golden in colour and very different in flavour from light sesame oil sold in health food stores. It is usually used as a flavouring at the end of cooking. Just a few drops are sufficient.

Shrimp   A staple of South-East Asia, these tiny dried shrimps give flavour and protein value to many dishes. They should be a good, bright salmon pink colour and not rock hard to the touch. Even though sold in airtight polythene packets, it is best to refrigerate them. Soak in hot water for 10 minutes and drain before using. Simmer whole with soups or pulverise to a floss and cook with chilli for hot sambals. If the recipe specifies 'very tiny dried shrimp', there is another variety which is hardly larger than a sliver of fingernail. This can be added straight from the packet.

Sambal ulek (oelek)   *See* **Chillies**.

Shrimp paste   Made from dried shrimp, this is powerful but if used in tiny quantities makes a great difference in flavour. Sold in jars or blocks. Keeps indefinitely.

Tamarind   The fruit of a tropical tree, tamarind imparts acidity to many dishes. It is sold dried (the truest flavour), puréed and instant. Some puréed or instant tamarind products can be too acid or salty. Check the product's strength before adding and adjust quantity accordingly.

Turmeric   A rhizome of the ginger family with bright yellow flesh under a brown skin. Mostly available dried and ground, it is a component in commercial curry blends.

Vietnamese mint   Not really a mint, but *polygonum odoratum*. It has a tingly, faintly hot flavour. Available at Asian markets and some nurseries. Substitute mint.

Index

Accompaniments
 Bombay duck chilli fry 74
 Burmese cucumber relish 44
 chilli oil pickle 73
 cucumber raita 72
 fried eggplant pickle 70
 garnished pappadams 69
 onion sambal 74
 Parsi wedding pickle 71
 see also Breads, Sauces

Beef
 chilli with snow peas 39
 frikkadels 33
 Indonesian curry 42
 Masaman curry 51
 Smoore 45
 spicy satay with peanut sauce 41
 spicy schnitzel 46
Bread
 chapatis 60
 parathas 62
 puris 61

Chicken
 biriani 66
 braised Mandarin 19
 chilli noodles 68
 country captain 16
 curried livers 26
 dopiaza 18
 Hunan-style 17
 Indonesian soup 15
 Maharashtra 22
 one-hundred almond curry 25
 satay 24
 Sri Lanka curry 24
 Thai and galangal soup 13
 with chilli radish 20
 with peanut sauce 21
Crab curry 10
Curry
 Burmese pork 43
 chicken livers 26
 crab 10
 duck vindaloo 31
 fish, Thai red 3
 forequarter chops 38
 green, of duck with sawtaw nuts 27
 Indonesian beef 42

lamb 40
liver 36
Masaman 51
meat and potato 37
one-hundred almond 25
pastes, *see* Spice mixtures
pork and liver 48
potato with tamarind 55
Punjabi meatball 34
Sir Lanka chicken
Sri Lankan fish with tamarind 2
Thai chicken with basil 14
Thai eggplant 56
white vegetable 58

Duck
 green curry with sawtaw nuts 27
 quick barbecue-style 29
 vindaloo 31
 with potatoes and onions 32

Egg sambal, Indonesian 23

Fish
 in chilli bean sauce 8
 Sri Lankan curry with tamarind 2
 Thai steamed pudding 4
 Thai red curry 3

Lamb
 and potato curry 37
 biriani 66
 curried forequarter chops 38
 curry 40
 jhal farezi 49
 koftas in saffron sauce 35
 Punjabi meatball curry 34
 rice cooked in stock 65
Liver
 and pork curry 48
 curried chicken 26
 curry 36

Meats 33–51
Mussels, Thai stuffed 9

Noodles
 chilli chicken 68
 fried rice 67

Pancakes, Mandarin 30
Pork
    and liver curry 48
    Burmese curry 43
    spicy satay with peanut sauce 41
    spicy spareribs 47
    steamed, layered 50
Poultry 12–32
Prawns
    chilli 5
    devilled 1
    hot-sour soup 6
    Thai with basil 7

Rice
    biriani 66
    cooked in meat stock 65
    steamed short grain 63
    steamed long grain 64

Satay, spicy with peanut sauce 41
Sauces
    chilli bean 8
    garlic chilli 76
    peanut 75

Seafood 1–11
Soup
    galangal and Thai chicken 13
    hot-sour prawn 6
    Indonesian chicken 15
Spice mixtures
    Ceylon curry powder 79
    fragrant garam masala 78
    garam masala 78
    green masala paste 84
    Masaman curry paste 83
    panch phora 77
    pepper and coriander paste 82
    Thai red curry paste 81

Turkey, devilled 28

Vegetables
    bean sayur 54
    deep fried green beans 53
    Ma Po Dou Fu 57
    potato curry with tamarind 55
    spicy mashed potatoes 52
    Thai eggplant curry 56
    white vegetable curry 58